A Midsummer Night's Dream

TITANIA AND BOTTOM

Illustration by Arthur Rackham from William Shakespeare,
A Midsummer Night's Dream (London: Heinemann, 1908).

A Midsummer Night's Dream

Helen Hackett

in association with
The British Council

For Steve
with love

© Copyright 1997 by Helen Hackett

First published in 1997 by Northcote House Publishers Ltd, Plymbridge House,
Estover Road, Plymouth PL6 7PY, United Kingdom.
Tel: +44 (0) 1752 202368. Fax: +44 (0) 1752 202330.

British Library Cataloguing-in-Publication Data
A catalogue record for this book is available from the British Library

ISBN 0 7463 0754 3

Typeset by Kestrel Data, Exeter
Printed and bound in the United Kingdom

Contents

Illustrations

Illustration acknowledgements

The author and the publishers gratefully acknowledge the following for supplying illustrations and granting permission for their use:

Cover detail and *Frontispiece:* copyright © The Estate of Arthur Rackham reproduced by permission of Reed Books; *Plate 1:* The Board of Trustees of the Victoria & Albert Museum, London; *Plate 2:* by courtesy of the Marquess of Salisbury; *Plates 3, 4, 5, 6, 7:* The Shakespeare Birthplace Trust, Stratford-upon-Avon; *Plate 8:* British Film Institute, London, © 1935 Turner Entertainment Co., USA. All Rights Reserved.

Acknowledgements

I would like to thank Isobel Armstrong for inviting me to write this book. I would also like to express my appreciation of the interest and support of my colleagues and students in the English Department of University College London. In particular, Kathy Metzenthin, John Sutherland and David Trotter gave assistance with computer equipment; and John Allen of UCL Library and René Weis helped me to obtain books which I needed. I am especially grateful to Valerie Williamson, Sarah Wintle and Henry Woudhuysen for their generosity in reading the typescript and sharing their extremely helpful responses with me. The book's remaining deficiencies are of course my own responsibility.

Steve Hackett has had to live with the simultaneous gestation of this book and a baby. He has been an astute reader and a patient listener, and has helped in more ways than I can list here. This book is for him.

Introduction

A Midsummer Night's Dream was written and first performed some
time in 1595 or 1596 (Holland, pp. 110–12). It therefore falls around
the early-to-middle period of Shakespeare's career: later than early
comedies like *The Comedy of Errors* (1592–4) and *The Taming of the
Shrew* (1593–4), but a few years earlier than the so-called 'golden'
comedies, *As You Like It* (1599) and *Twelfth Night* (1601–2; all dates
from *The Riverside Shakespeare*). It is a romantic comedy, inter-
weaving the vicissitudes in love of four couples: the two pairs
of young Athenian lovers, Hermia and Lysander, Helena and
Demetrius; Theseus, Duke of Athens, and his new bride
Hippolyta, the conquered Amazon Queen; and Oberon and
Titania, the Fairy King and Queen.

The play thus presents us with three different stages of courtship
and marriage. Hermia, her friend Helena, and their two lovers
epitomize youth, a phase when different possibilities in love can
be explored in ways sometimes playful, sometimes painful. At the
beginning of the play Hermia and Lysander love each other, and
Helena loves Demetrius, but he has rejected her and is courting
Hermia. Hermia's father, Egeus, approves of Demetrius and wants
to compel Hermia to marry him. In the course of the play we will
see first Lysander then Demetrius switch their affection to Helena,
producing comic chaos but also increasingly bitter discord among
all four characters, until finally Lysander switches back to Hermia
and the lovers fall neatly into two pairs. This plot of exchanges
of partner has a schematic, formal quality, like a game or a dance;
yet at the same time it enables expressions of the youthful agonies
of love, such as affection obstructed by parents, as suffered by
Hermia and Lysander, and unrequited passion, as endured by
Helena.

1

Theseus and Hippolyta are more mature characters, each of them accustomed to command and to their independence; but as they prepare for their marriage, a marriage which follows abruptly upon their enmity in war, they must negotiate ways to become a harmoniously united couple. Oberon and Titania are already married, but, at the opening of the play, are violently at odds with one another; they therefore represent a middle stage of marriage, in which the initial romance may have worn off and descended into acrimony and a contest for dominance. A fresh start is effected by comic means, through an enchantment instigated by Oberon whereby Titania falls in love with Bottom, a weaver. Bottom is an inappropriate partner for the Fairy Queen as a mortal, a humble craftsman, and something of a buffoon, but beyond this he has also fallen victim to the mischievous magic of Puck, Oberon's hobgoblin accomplice, and consequently is unwittingly sporting the head of an ass. After a period of absurd infatuation with this semi-bestial creature Titania awakes to a renewed affection for her husband.

These different strands of plot are bound together not only by the theme of love and marriage, but also by the recurrent intervention of magic. Bottom is transformed by a spell, Titania is made to fall in love with him by the application of a love-charm to her eyes, and the same love-charm brings about the reversals of affection of the four young lovers. As can be seen from all these episodes, fairy-magic in this play is a wayward and unpredictable force. Sometimes it goes wrong, as when Puck mistakenly makes Lysander rather than Demetrius switch his love from Hermia to Helena, multiplying rather than resolving the conflicts among the foursome. At other times, though, it is motivated by a simple delight in stirring up mischief and in practical jokes against oblivious mortals, as in Puck's transformation of Bottom's head, or, later, the way he mimics each of the four young lovers to lead them on through the night like a will-o'-the-wisp, confusing and exhausting them.

The fairies in the play are in some ways rather like the gods in ancient Greek or Roman mythology, in that they possess superhuman powers and yet are subject to human emotions like jealousy, passion and revenge; and when they act on these emotions, any mortals who happen to cross their paths can find themselves helplessly embroiled in the consequences. Like the pagan gods, the fairies occupy a different plane of action from that of mortals, yet at the same time have the ability to intervene in the affairs of humans, affecting them in ways which are baffling and mystifying. This often makes the fairies seem like personifications of the kinds of mysterious and ungovernable external forces – such as fate, or luck, or nature, or love – which can override the attempts of humans to plan and control our own destinies.

Such forces are unsusceptible to rational control, and the sense that they are unleashed and allowed free play in this drama is enhanced by its setting in a dream-world where anything seems possible. Of course, the very title of the play presents its whole action as a dream, encouraging us to enjoy it as a temporary space of fantasy and release. This in turn invites us to contemplate the theatre, and art in general, as realms where the imagination can work wonders. Increasingly, as the play goes on, it comes to reflect self-consciously upon the powers, and also the limitations, of its own dramatic medium.

These are some of the aspects of *A Midsummer Night's Dream* which this book will consider. Its overall aim is to explore how we might think about *A Midsummer Night's Dream* now, in the wake of all the recent diverse and fertile developments in Shakespeare criticism. Feminist criticism is especially illuminating of this play which is so concerned with marriage enforced or based on love, with female power in conflict with male authority, and with female friendship; these topics are all addressed in my first three chapters. New historicist critics have shown how fruitful it is to read texts in terms of both their construction by, and their contribution to, the political and cultural currents in play at the time of their composition; this approach is particularly explored in chapter 2. Chapter 3 examines the play in relation to genre-theory; chapter 4 discusses how psychoanalytical thought has affected readings and performances of this self-styled dream. Chapters 4 and 5 also consider how stagings and adaptations of the play can throw light upon diverse and even conflicting interpretations. Throughout, the fluid and creative intertextuality of the play is kept in view: that is, the extent to which it is woven out of prior texts, and has itself in turn inspired and contributed to the weaving of later texts. Throughout, my hope is that I have used none of these approaches in a rigid

1

Metamorphoses and the Moon

The action, the imagery and the themes of *A Midsummer Night's Dream* all revolve around different kinds of change. A 'little western flower' is transformed into a love-charm (II. i. 166), while Bottom is 'translated' into an ass (III. i. 113); Oberon and Titania fight over a 'little changeling boy' (II. i. 120), while Demetrius and Lysander switch their romantic attachments back and forth between Hermia and Helena. The description of the contested Indian boy as a 'changeling' alludes to the folk-myth that fairies may steal away a human baby for whom they substitute one of their own kind in the cradle. However, in the sixteenth and seventeenth centuries the word 'changeling' could also have the wider sense of anyone who changes either their nature or their allegiances, as in the title of Thomas Middleton's and William Rowley's play *The Changeling*, 1623: there it principally refers to the female protagonist Beatrice-Joanna, who switches between three male partners in the course of the play. In this sense, Demetrius, Lysander and even Titania herself are changelings.

David Marshall points out some more of the multiple resonances of the term 'changeling' in the *Dream*, where characters not only change but are exchanged as commodities: 'In becoming a disfigured substitute for Titania's changeling boy, [Bottom] becomes both a changeling for himself (a monster left in his own place) and a changeling for the changeling (which Titania has been tricked into exchanging)' (1982, in Bloom, pp. 112–13). Hermia too is treated as a property which her father wishes to exchange with the suitor of his choice in a quasi-commercial transaction. As Egeus bluntly puts it, 'As she is mine, I may dispose of her' (I. i. 42), and Lysander's diversion of her affection is a theft, a crime against property (I. i. 32, IV. i. 155). She is a vivid example of what has been called the 'traffic in women' between fathers and husbands which binds patriarchal societies together (Rubin).

Change, then, can have the sense of changed affection and of exchange; but it can also have more lyrical connotations of transformation, of changes wrought by magical and mysterious outside forces. This is what Shakespeare extensively explores on other levels of the play, addressing the transmutative powers of dreams, of love, and of the imagination. Such ideas are often articulated in the play through the confusion of the senses: as Bottom puts it on awaking,

> I have had a most rare vision. I have had a dream past the wit of man to say what dream it was . . . The eye of man hath not heard, the ear of man hath not seen, man's hand is not able to taste, his tongue to conceive, nor his heart to report what my dream was (IV. i. 201–10).

Here Bottom both comically and profoundly scrambles a biblical allusion: St Paul writes in 1. Corinthians 2:9–10, 'the eye hath not seen, and the ear hath not heard, neither have entered into the heart of man, the things which God hath prepared for them that love him' (Bishops' Bible, 1568; Holland, IV. i. 208–11n). The moment highlights the way in which humour – here, characteristically for Bottom, the humour of malapropism and verbal misplacing – is seamlessly integrated with the more thought-provoking themes of the play.

This theme of transformation is also articulated through another kind of allusion: extensive echoing of Ovid's *Metamorphoses*. This classical work was a kind of comic epic of change; its very title literally means 'changes of form'. It narrates transformative encounters, especially erotic encounters, between gods and mortals, and presents these events as mythological explanations of changeful phenomena in the natural world. Bottom's bestial transmutation and penetration into the secluded bower of the Fairy Queen recall, in comic form, Ovid's story of Actaeon's tragic transformation into a deer when he interrupted the private bath of the goddess Diana (Ovid, III. 138–252). In addition, the story of *Pyramus and Thisbe* which forms the subject of the play presented by Bottom and his friends, the mechanicals, at the wedding celebration in Act V of *A Midsummer Night's Dream*, derives directly from the *Metamorphoses*. There are other resonances of Ovid throughout the *Dream*: when Helena tells

Demetrius that 'The story shall be changed:/ Apollo flies, and Daphne holds the chase', an Ovidian tale is at once invoked, and itself reshaped in the process. Whereas in Ovid it is usually libidinous male gods who pursue mortal maidens like Daphne, Helena's indefatigable desire inverts the traditional roles (II. i. 230–1).

Ovid could be read in English in Shakespeare's time in Arthur Golding's translation of 1567 (although we know that Shakespeare also read the original Latin; see below). The mechanicals' script for *Pyramus and Thisbe* draws on Golding's version, whose innate though unintended comic potential can be demonstrated from a few brief quotations. When Pyramus finds Thisbe's blood-stained mantle,

> Receive thou my blood too (quoth he) and therewithall he drew
> His sword, the which among his guts he thrust, and by and by
> Did draw it from the bleeding wound beginning for to die
> And cast himself upon his back. The blood did spin on high
> As when a conduit pipe is cracked, the water bursting out
> Doth shoot itself a great way off and pierce the air about.

Thisbe in turn discovers his corpse:

> She beat her breast, she shriekèd out, she tare her golden hairs,
> And taking him between her arms did wash his wounds with tears.

She cries out:

> Alas what chance my *Pyramus* hath parted thee and me?
> Make answer O my *Pyramus*: it is thy *Thisb'*, even she
> Whom thou dost love most heartily that speaketh unto thee.

After more lines of monologue,

> This said, she took the sword yet warm with slaughter of her love
> And setting it beneath her breast, did to her heart it shove.
> (Brooks, Appendix I. 7, pp. 151–3)

The image of the burst pipe is original to Ovid:

> ut iacuit resupinus humo, cruor emicat alte,
> non aliter quam cum vitiato fistula plumbo
> scinditur et tenui stridente foramine longas
> eiaculatur aquas atque ictibus aera rumpit.

As he lay stretched upon the earth the spouting blood leaped high;
just as when a pipe has broken at a weak spot in the lead and through
the small hissing aperture sends spurting forth long streams of water,
cleaving the air with its jets. (IV. 121–4)

Here in Ovid, the combination of graphic violence with a somewhat bathetic image drawn from plumbing produces a
sophisticated unfixity of tone, poised between high tragedy and
an implied ripple of ironic authorial humour at the excessiveness
of the spectacle. In Golding, however, the translation of the
scene into a jog-trot metre, and diction which would have been
antiquated by the time Shakespeare was writing the *Dream* in
the 1590s, tip the balance towards absurdity and produce an
irresistible opportunity for parody.

Golding wrote in 'fourteeners', a popular metre for English
poetry in the 1560s. It consists of fourteen-syllable lines, compared
with which the ten-syllabled iambic pentameter, which had
become the favoured English metre by the time Shakespeare was
writing, is at once more concise, more fluid and more like the
rhythms of natural speech. The longer lines of fourteeners require
Golding to pad out his writing with rather flabby and banal
phrases like 'by and by', 'beginning for to die' (meaning simply
'dying') and 'thee and me' (for 'us'). In his play, Quince proposes
to adopt Golding's metre when he announces that his Prologue
will be written in 'eight and six' (III. i. 21–2), that is, fourteeners
broken up into shorter lines. In fact, some of the most climactic
passages of the final performance of *Pyramus and Thisbe* are broken
up even further, into lines of four, four and six syllables, though
this too adds up to fourteeners under another guise and supplies
a kind of comic homage to Golding:

> Come tears, confound;
> Out sword, and wound
> The pap of Pyramus.
> Ay, that left pap,
> Where heart doth hop.
> Thus die I: thus, thus, thus.

> (V. i. 289–94)

The breaking up of the fourteeners into these shorter rhymed lines
demonstrates how very easily they can subside into the doggerel

manner of light verse rather than the intended grand, high tone of tragedy.

Although comic success is obviously far from what Golding envisaged, it is a kind of tribute to his unknowing comic genius that the Golding-inspired performance of *Pyramus and Thisbe* usually produces hilarity among modern audiences, even though they may have no knowledge of either Ovid or Golding and may be unaware that this is a specific literary parody. Partly this is because productions of the *Dream* often include a good deal of slapstick stage-business in the mechanicals' appearances; but this is by no means out of keeping with the text, whereas comic scenes in other Shakespeare plays are often felt to need the grafting on of gratuitous visual humour to make them even slightly amusing to a modern audience. In any case, it is usually not just the slapstick of *Pyramus and Thisbe* which raises laughs, but the ridiculously over-inflated language too. Shakespeare is undoubtedly accomplished at making Golding even funnier, but he is accentuating absurdity which was already there in his source material.

In Ovid's original *Metamorphoses*, the passage of time was often denoted by reference to the phases of the moon (Purdon, 1974, in Price, p. 170). This was highly appropriate since the moon itself was a symbol of change, in its passage through monthly cycles culminating in the transition from old moon to new, and in its association with the ebb and flow of the tides. Even more so than the *Metamorphoses*, *A Midsummer Night's Dream* is presided over by this mutable heavenly body. Examples are abundant, ranging from Oberon's ringing salutation, 'Ill met by moonlight, proud Titania' (II. i. 60), to Starveling's notable performance as Moonshine. The motif is firmly established in the very opening moments of the *Dream*, where we are told that the marriage-day of Theseus and Hippolyta has been determined by the lunar calendar and cannot take place until the new moon comes in. Theseus complains,

> O, methinks, how slow
> This old moon wanes! She lingers my desires
> Like to a stepdame or a dowager
> Long withering out a young man's revenue.

> (I. i. 3–6)

9

The moon, here as at most points through the play, is emphatically personified as female, and for Theseus she is like a sterile and spiteful old woman whose refusal to die denies him his promised pleasures.

We might wonder why the stated delay of four days is necessary; if Theseus is so impatient, why should he not, as Duke of Athens and Hippolyta's conqueror, set the date as early as he pleases? The question seems even more perplexing in view of the inconsistency of the time-scheme here with that of the rest of the play, in which the lovers flee to the woods from this scene at Theseus's court 'tomorrow night' (I. i. 164, 223, 247), then wake from the adventures of that night to find it already the day of the ducal wedding (IV. i. 131–5, 184). Conflicting time schemes are common in Shakespearean drama; *Othello* is perhaps the most striking example. As in that play, so also in the case of *A Midsummer Night's Dream* an explanation can be found in the different purposes served by the variant impressions of time at different points in the play: Theseus's complaint about the four days dramatizes the urgency of his desire, whereas near the end of the play the sense must be conveyed of waking to a new world from a single transformative night. Other pragmatic explanations for the four days can also be adduced: time is needed to arrange the 'pomp . . . triumph, and . . . revelling' to mark the wedding (I. i. 19), and for Theseus to win Hippolyta's heart as well as the body he has conquered with his sword (I. i. 16–18). Hippolyta seems more sanguine than Theseus about the delay:

> Four days will quickly steep themselves in night;
> Four nights will quickly dream away the time;
> And then the moon, like to a silver bow
> New bent in heaven, shall behold the night
> Of our solemnities.
>
> (I. i. 7–11)

Critics, and productions, have been divided as to whether Hippolyta is calmly compliant with the marriage or furiously resentful, as befits the Queen of the Amazons, an aggressively anti-male nation of women, who has been only very recently subdued by force. For G. K. Hunter the tone of her exchange with Theseus is a 'combination of romance and merriment' which epitomizes 'a settled and rational state of loving' (1962, in Price,

p. 123); for C. L. Barber, 'Theseus looks towards the hour with masculine impatience, Hippolyta with a woman's happy willingness to dream away the time' (p. 125). David Marshall, however, retorts, 'I fail to see any sign of either happiness or willingness in Hippolyta's response to Theseus' expression of impatience' (1982, in Bloom, p. 92). In recent productions Hippolyta has often expressed defiance in her tone and gestures, including, later in the first scene, manifest displeasure at Theseus's endorsement of the harsh patriarchal law in support of Egeus against his daughter Hermia and her desire to choose her own husband. This reading seems to be supported by Theseus's uneasy inquiry when, after sternly admonishing Hermia, he turns back to his betrothed to ask, 'what cheer, my love?' (I. i. 122; see Holland, p. 51). Indeed, interpretations of Hippolyta as a recalcitrant bride-to-be are more than just recent feminist contrivances. The film of the play made by Max Reinhardt and William Dieterle as early as 1935 showed her clearly as a dejected alien captive (Halio, pp. 86–7). In Shakespeare's own time, the iconography of Amazons (that is, the conventions of the visual images and descriptions by which they were represented) associated them with female autonomy and unruly opposition to male power (Olson, 1957, in Price, pp. 79–80; Holland, pp. 49–51).

For the moment, however, in this first scene, Theseus, the conqueror of the Amazon Queen, seems himself to be subject to a higher female power, the moon. In general, as I mentioned in my Introduction, this is very much a play in which mysterious forces, elusive of rational control, are shown irresistibly turning human events and feelings aside from their planned courses. Love, dreams and the imagination all participate in this effect, and, as I suggested, the fairies themselves can be understood as personifications of invisible forces of nature and of fortune which override the attempts of humans to govern our own lives. The moon too, in the light of traditional superstitions, possessed just such inexplicable but incontestable powers. Richard Wilson points out that

> [m]ention of the lunar cycle is a reminder . . . of the belief that, as governess of menstruation and tides, a waning moon brought blood, tears, sterility and death, so that, as John Aubrey warned, 'it is not good to undertake any business at the last period of her revolution'. (p. 14)

The reason for the delay of the wedding may be this belief that an old moon is unpropitious. Reinforcing this, though, it may not be fanciful to suggest that the waning of the moon coincides with Hippolyta's own menstrual period, an interval of about four days which would constrain an eager bridegroom to wait. The processes of women's bodies are another kind of incomprehensible but incontrovertible natural force: mysterious to men, unsusceptible to external government, and cyclical like the moon, the fact of menstruation is perhaps the delay which Theseus must accept and submit to. In Elizabethan English, menstrual blood was called 'flowers' (*OED* 2b; Montrose, p. 333, n. 31). In the original Ovidian story of Pyramus and Thisbe the scattered blood of the lovers' mortal wounds dyes the berries of the nearby mulberry bush from white to purple (Brooks, pp. 151–3); this transmutation is in turn transposed by Shakespeare to the flower which becomes Oberon's love-charm as a consequence of having been pierced by the 'love-shaft' of Cupid, god of desire. It was 'Before, milk-white; now, purple with love's wound', and is accordingly empowered to awaken immediate desire in those whom it touches (II. i. 159, 167). The motif seems to figure the blood-stains both of menstrual flowers and of deflowering. Likewise, perhaps Theseus has to wait for menstrual flowers to cease, in their own time, before he can deflower his bride.

The change of the moon certainly has another direct association with female bodily change in this opening scene: it will mark Hippolyta's transition from virginity to wifehood. Hippolyta's simile for the new moon as 'like to a silver bow/ New bent in heaven' invokes its mythological association with the divine huntress Diana, goddess of virginity (I. i. 9–10). Diana's hunting weapons symbolized her chastity, her impregnability to sexual advances, just as did martial instruments in the iconography of Amazons. Hippolyta, like Diana, wears buskins, shin-guards worn for protection in hunting or battle and an emblem of the virginal warrior-woman (II. i. 71). At the same time, however, the bow is an attribute not just of Diana, but also of Cupid, the mischievous god of love; we will hear shortly of how his arrow was loosed 'smartly from his bow' when it hit the little western flower (II. i. 159). Puck, who is a Cupid-like figure in his boyishness and his practical-joking intervention in matters of love, flies 'Swifter than arrow from the Tartar's bow' (III. ii. 101).

Moreover, in the fashionable Elizabethan love poetry written in imitation of the Italian poet Petrarch, the male lover pursuing his mistress was frequently figured as a hunter chasing his 'deer/dear', as in Sir Thomas Wyatt's sonnet 'Whoso list to hunt' (Norbrook and Woudhuysen, p. 182, no. 54), or Edmund Spenser's sonnet 'Lyke as a huntsman after weary chace' (*Amoretti* LXVII, Spenser, *Shorter Poems*, p. 640). In Hippolyta's image of the bow for the new moon, then, Diana's bow, figuring female sexual autonomy and virginal intactness, is overlaid with Cupid's bow and the bow of the Petrarchan lover, figuring male desire and penetration, a blurring of associations which aptly represents the fact that the change of the moon will mark the Amazon's transmutation from absolute virgin queen to wifely queen consort.

The association of the moon with Diana, and thereby with female chastity, is sustained at later points in the play. Theseus warns Hermia that if she chooses the nunnery over death or Demetrius, she will expend her life as a 'barren sister . . ./ Chanting faint hymns to the cold fruitless moon' (I. i. 72–3). Cupid's arrow, in Oberon's account of the origin of the floral love-charm, was intended for an ethereal 'imperial vot'ress', but her invulnerability to desire caused the arrow to be 'Quenched in the chaste beams of the wat'ry moon' (II. i. 162–3). Such emphasis on the virginal aspect of the moon is appropriate to a play which concerns the period immediately preceding the weddings of its three heroines, Hippolyta, Hermia and Helena. However, the moon has a further, double aptness to this theme: it also had other, directly opposite, iconographical associations, with love and fertility. It is of course the presiding heavenly body of the night, and the night is the time for love: hence it is by moonlight that Lysander has wooed Hermia and 'stol'n the impression of her fantasy' (I. i. 32); hence too it is by moonshine that Pyramus and Thisbe meet secretly at 'Ninny's tomb'. Titania speaks ambiguously when she says that

> The moon, methinks, looks with a wat'ry eye,
> And when she weeps, weeps every little flower,
> Lamenting some enforcèd chastity.
>
> (III. i. 188–90)

The moon may be weeping for chastity which has been forced in the sense of violated, like the Ovidian story of Philomel 'so rudely forc'd' by Tereus (Eliot, *The Waste Land*, III. 204; Ovid, VI. 412–674); or 'enforcèd' may mean 'imposed', a chastity forced on a woman who does not wish to remain a virgin, just as Theseus threatens to enforce Hermia to be a nun. This verbal ambiguity accords with the richly ambivalent iconographical properties of the moon as patron both of female virginity, and of love and fertility, and so accentuates its aptness in a play in which the heroines stand on the brink between maidenhood and marriage.

The moon has yet another kind of doubleness in the play: just as there is an inconsistency between the four days' interval and the overnight action of the play, the exact phase of the moon is given differently at different points. The first scene tells us that we are between the old and new moons, that is, at a time when no moon or only a very thin moon is shining; yet Titania is 'Ill met by moonlight' on her way to lead 'moonlight revels' (II. i. 60, 141), the mechanicals' rehearsal is by moonlight (I. ii. 91–2), their almanac tells them that the moon will shine brightly enough on the night of their performance to illuminate the scene through an open casement (III. i. 43–54), and 'the wolf behowls the moon' on the night which closes the play (V. i. 363; Wilson, p. 14). Again, different points in the action require the invocation of different properties of the moon: the cusp between the old and new moons is appropriate to the moment between courtship and marriage, and frustration with the old moon symbolizes Theseus's impatient desire; but the full moon is needed to preside over the action of the play because of the magical light which it casts, a light by which everything appears slightly different from usual.

The moonlit night is a setting where lovers can pursue their forbidden desires in relative secrecy; and in other ways too it is a setting where anything can happen, a time of dreams, of the distortion of conscious perceptions, of the inversion of the waking world. Elizabethans believed that the influence of the moon induced madness or 'lunacy', a term which literally means 'a state brought on by the moon'; hence Theseus groups together '[t]he lunatic, the lover and the poet' as susceptible to wild imaginings (V. i. 7). The changefulness which the moon exemplifies could be renewing and transformative, but it could also stand for un-reliability and irrationality: Juliet, for instance, forestalls Romeo, 'O, swear not by the moon, th'inconstant moon,/ That monthly changes in her circled orb' (II. ii. 109–10). The heavenly body of the night could preside over occult practices, such that in classical mythology the moon-goddess had three aspects: the chaste Diana was her persona when she appeared on earth; in heaven her title was Luna, Cynthia or Phoebe; and in Hades, the underworld, she adopted the guise of Hecate, goddess of magic, ghosts and witchcraft. This triformity and occult aspect are what Puck refers to when he speaks of 'we fairies that do run/ By the triple Hecate's team' (V. i. 374–5). Hecate's dark associations included sinister and threatening aspects of female sexuality.

The name Titania was linked to these diverse aspects of the moon. Ovid referred to Diana as Titania in his narrative of her encounter with Actaeon (*Metamorphoses*, III. 173); it applied to her as sister of the Titan Helios, the sun god, and granddaughter of the Titan Coeus. Hecate too, though, was a 'Titanian' goddess, as daughter of the Titan Perses (Brewer, p. 541). Shakespeare's Titania is obviously a less malignant and threatening figure than Hecate, but she is obliquely associated with her as a Queen of the Night who works charms and spells and can be spiteful and wilful if not propitiated. Ovid also used the name Titania for Circe, the enchantress who seduced unwary mariners with her charms and then transformed them into beasts (*Metamorphoses*, XIV. 382, 438; Foakes, p. 7). Her powers as a shape-changer have obvious relevance to *A Midsummer Night's Dream*, although here again Shakespeare reshapes the Ovidian story: instead of a female seductress who exploits men's sexual desires in order to to enthrall, humiliate and bestialize them, we see in Shakespeare's Titania a woman with magical powers who is herself enthralled and humiliated by her passion for a beast. His use of the name Titania tells us that he had read the *Metamorphoses* in Latin as well as Golding's English, since Golding never uses the form 'Titania', translating it instead into phrases like 'Titan's daughter' (Holland, p. 32).

Titania's story can be seen as an enactment of the enforced humbling of female power (Berry, pp. 143–6), as can Hippolyta's subordination to Theseus; after all, despite Theseus's apparent subjugation to female forces in the opening scene, Hippolyta is his conquest and captive, and his enforced deference to the waning moon is temporary and brief. In modern productions, attention is often drawn to this parallel theme in the two plots by a doubling of roles, whereby a single actress plays Hippolyta and Titania and a single actor plays Theseus and Oberon (see Chapter 4 below). Yet these plots which show as proper and necessary the subordination of regal women to the higher authorities of men were written by Shakespeare at a time when England was under the rule of a queen, Elizabeth I. This queen was not only unmarried and therefore absolute and autonomous; she was also frequently represented in literature as a moon-goddess. Moreover, she even appears personally in her moon-goddess persona in this very play. My next chapter will consider what connections can be drawn between these intriguing facts, and how they may illuminate *A Midsummer Night's Dream*.

2

The Play in Its Time: Female Power

As I said in my Introduction, *A Midsummer Night's Dream* can be dated to 1595–6; it thus belongs to the final decade of the reign of Elizabeth I, who died in 1603. Moon-imagery was extremely common in the literature of this decade, especially in panegyric (that is, the literature of praise and celebration of the monarch). Diana, goddess of chastity, was obviously a fitting persona for the Virgin Queen, an aptness reinforced by the fact that Elizabeth's favourite pastime was hunting. The moon could also, as ruler of the tidal oceans, be adopted as a symbol of England's burgeoning imperial aspirations. For example, in 1591, during a royal progress, entertainments were provided for the Queen and her court at Elvetham; they included marine pageants on a pool constructed in the shape of a crescent moon, and Elizabeth was hailed as 'Fair Cynthia the wide Ocean's Empress' (Nichols, vol. 3, p. 111).

George Peele, in *The Honour of the Garter*, 1593, represents the procession of the Queen and the Knights of the Garter at Windsor as a dream-vision of the rising moon and stars in the night sky:

> Under the glorious spreading wings of Fame,
> I saw a Virgin Queen, attired in white,
> Leading with her a sort of goodly knights
>
> ....
> She was the sovereign of the knights she led.
> Her face methought I knew: as if the same,
> The same great Empress that we here enjoy,
> Had climbed the clouds, and been in person there;
> To whom the earth, the sea, and elements
> Auspicious are.

> > (Peele, vol. 1, pp. 245–59, ll. 319–31)

The poem demonstrates why moon-imagery became so prevalent in panegyric: it rendered Elizabeth ethereal, radiant and quasi-divine. Similarly, George Chapman, in *The Shadow of Night*, 1594, represented Elizabeth as the rising moon-goddess, 'Enchantress-like, decked in disparent lawn,/ Circled with charms and incantations' (Chapman, 'Hymnus in Noctem', ll. 395–6).

Such poetic visions are closely echoed in Act II of *A Midsummer Night's Dream*, when Oberon describes to Puck his vision of an 'imperial vot'ress' whose invulnerability to Cupid's arrow resulted in the transformation of the flower into a love-charm. He recounts:

> I saw, but thou couldst not,
> Flying between the cold moon and the earth
> Cupid, all armed. A certain aim he took
> At a fair vestal thronèd by the west,
> And loosed his love-shaft smartly from his bow
> As it should pierce a hundred thousand hearts.
> But I might see young Cupid's fiery shaft
> Quenched in the chaste beams of the wat'ry moon,
> And the imperial vot'ress passèd on,
> In maiden meditation, fancy-free.
>
> (II. i. 155–64)

The terms 'vestal' 'thronèd by the west' and 'imperial', combined with the association with the chaste moon, were all conventional to poetic representations of Elizabeth, and clearly indicate that this passage participates in contemporary royal panegyric. Just like Peele's and Chapman's moon-goddesses, this superhuman figure glides translucently across the sky.

At another point in Chapman's poem, he exhorted the regal moon-goddess:

> Ascend thy chariot, and make earth admire
> Thy old swift changes, made a young fixed prime;
> O let thy beauty scorch the wings of time.
> (Chapman, 'Hymnus in Cynthiam', ll. 16–18)

Here we see a further reason why lunar imagery became increasingly popular for Elizabeth in the 1590s: as she grew older, its cyclical connotations could be used to suggest powers of infinite self-renewal, infinite youthfulness, and even goddess-like immortality. A song in praise of the Queen published in John Dowland's *Third Book of Songs*, 1603, declared:

> See the moon
> That ever in one change doth grow
> Yet still the same; and she is so;
> So, so, so, and only so.
>
> (Fellowes, p. 482)

However, these celebrations of Elizabeth's immunity to change and mortality were of course idealizations, and there is other evidence that as the 1590s progressed she was visibly in decline. She was in her sixties, and as her public image in portraiture as well as poetry became ever more perfect and idealized, a 'mask of youth' (Plates 1 and 2), it was increasingly removed from, and arguably compensatory for, her ageing physical reality (Strong, pp. 146–51; Hackett, pp. 179–80). A gathering consciousness of the imminence of her death, combined with the fact that the end of the century was near, gave an acute sense of impending transition, a feeling that the present era was waning and would shortly give way to a new start. On the one hand the prospect of change seems to have induced some anxiety and uncertainty; after all, most of Elizabeth's subjects had been born since her accession in 1558 – including Shakespeare, born in 1564 – and had therefore never known another monarch. On the other hand, though, there was also excitement at the prospect of a new beginning, and feverish rumours of Elizabeth's illness and demise were rife for more than a decade before her death. This atmosphere created a widespread preoccupation with mutability – that is, the processes of change through time – which in turn gave impetus to the use of moon-imagery.

The eager anticipation of change was reinforced by the fact that Elizabeth's successor would be James of Scotland, returning England from what was, in terms of contemporary ideology and recent history, an anomalous and controversial state of rule by an unmarried and autonomous female, to the normal, 'natural' hierarchy which placed power in male hands (Hackett, ch. 6). Bishop Goodman (1583–1656), looking back in later life on the last years of Elizabeth's reign, said that 'in effect the people were very generally weary of an old woman's government' (Williams, p. 70; *DNB*, vol. 22, pp. 131–4). A favourite motif in elegies composed

Plate 1.
Elizabeth I, miniature by Nicholas Hilliard, c.1595 - 1600.
The Queen's face is the 'mask of youth' (she was in her sixties
at this time). She wears a crescent moon above her forehead, and
arrows of Diana, or of desire, on her ruff.

Plate 2.
Detail from the 'Rainbow' Portrait of Elizabeth I, attrib.
Marcus Gheeraerts the Younger, c.1600 - 03. Again, the Queen's face
is the 'mask of youth', and she wears a crescent moon at the top of
her head-dress.

when Elizabeth died was that of the feminine moon giving way to the more resplendent, masculine, dawning sun (Hackett, p. 220).

Impatience for change was compounded by various developing political discontents. At court, there was increasing frustration with Elizabeth's perceived wilfulness and fickleness of favour, traits which were attributed to her age and her femaleness. The more negative associations of the moon with mutability and dubious female powers were not therefore excluded from lunar representations of Elizabeth, even though, during her lifetime, they could of course only be invoked relatively indirectly. Her favourite Sir Walter Ralegh, in a poem entitled *The Ocean to Cynthia*, probably composed in 1592 when he was in severe disfavour, represents himself as the ocean – Elizabeth had nick-named him her 'Water' – helplessly drawn in and out of favour by her moon-like changeful influence. The poem begins as a celebration of the Queen and a declaration of love for her, then darkens as Ralegh complains of her arbitrary withdrawal of affection, and attributes it to the innate instability of womankind:

> So hath perfection which begat her mind
> Added thereto a change of fantasy,
> And left her the affections of her kind.
> (Norbrook and Woudhuysen, no. 21, ll. 209–11)

On top of Elizabeth's perceived fickleness towards individual courtiers, there was intense frustration with her cautious pragmatism in foreign policy and in government generally. Many of her younger male courtiers were impatient to pursue military glory in the Netherlands, Ireland and the New World. Her chief favourite of these later years, Robert Devereux, Earl of Essex, told the French ambassador in 1597 that 'they laboured under two things at this Court, delay and inconstancy, which proceeded chiefly from the sex of the Queen' (Hurault, p. 115). It is hard not to be reminded by this of Theseus's impatience with the old moon (see Wilson, p. 13); Elizabeth must have appeared to Essex very much like an aged stepmother or dowager constraining the full exercise of his virility while his youth passed by. I do not mean to suggest by this that Theseus and the old moon are direct allegorical personifications of Essex and Elizabeth, but that a contemporary sense of female power as an ageing and delaying force, as against male energy which chafes for action and progress, informs the gendered lunar iconography of Theseus's lines.

Essex's intimacy with Elizabeth was increasingly tempestuous. It was probably his exile from court in 1598, after he insolently turned his back on the Queen in a Privy Council meeting and she boxed his ears, which inspired 'A poem made on the Earl of Essex (being in disgrace with Queen Elizabeth)' by Henry Cuffe, his secretary and close supporter. It opens 'It was a time when silly bees could speak', and represents sycophantic courtiers as insects feeding on Elizabeth while the speaker malcontentedly looks on from the margins:

> I work on weeds when moon is in the wane,
>   Whilst all the swarm in sunshine taste the Rose;
> On black root fern I sit, and suck my bane,
>   Whilst on the Eglantine the rest repose;
>   Having too much they still repine for more,
>   And cloyed with sweetness surfeit on the store.
>
> (May, pp. 266–9)

The eglantine, the virginal white rose, was a conventional emblem for Elizabeth. Rather than glorifying it, Cuffe depicts those in favour as glutting and gorging themselves upon it, and conveys a powerful sense of general decadence and distemper all because the 'moon is in the wane'.

Moon-imagery was therefore invaluable to court poets of the 1590s precisely because of its doubleness, the moon's dark side as well as its radiant side, its changefulness as well as its infinite self-renewal. It could be used as a medium for what Annabel Patterson has called 'functional ambiguity': the expression of political criticism in coded terms, at once sufficiently veiled and ambivalent to evade the dangers of censorship and punishment, but at the same time soliciting the reader's implicit comprehension and collusion (Patterson, p. 18; and see Wilson).

Ambivalence about female rule also extended beyond the court. The desire for a more aggressive, 'masculine' foreign policy was shared on a popular level, and can be detected in Shakespeare's *Henry V*, not least in the choral passage celebrating Essex's expected triumphant return from his military campaign in Ireland (Act V, ll. 29–34). In addition, the mid-1590s were a period of outbreaks of plague, failed harvests, food shortages, and inflation.

Clearly, disease and failed crops were natural disasters, and could not be blamed on Elizabeth's rule; nevertheless, the privileges enjoyed by members of her court protected them from the consequences of those disasters, both in their ability to leave London for country estates when the plague struck, and in their possession of trade monopolies granted by the Crown which secured them from economic hardship at the expense of the poor. An Essex labourer in 1591, even before the worst period of deprivation, urged his fellow subjects to pray for a king, because 'the Queen is but a woman and ruled by noblemen, and the noblemen and gentlemen are all one, and the gentlemen and farmers will hold together so that the poor get nothing' (Haigh, p. 5).

Titania's speech about the cosmic reverberations of her conflict with Oberon may constitute a topical reference to the plague of 1593–4 and the exceptionally bad summer of 1594, as well as possibly the successive wet summers of 1595 and 1596:

> the green corn
> Hath rotted ere his youth attained a beard.
> ....
> The nine men's morris[1] is filled up with mud,
> And the quaint mazes in the wanton green
> For lack of tread are undistinguishable.
> ....
> the moon, the governess of floods,
> Pale in her anger, washes all the air,
> That rheumatic diseases do abound.
>
> (II. i. 94–5, 98–100, 103–5)

Simon Forman recorded in his journal for 1594 that

> June and July were very wet and wonderful cold like winter, [so] that the 10th day of July many did sit by the fire, it was so cold; and so was it in May and June . . . There were many great floods this summer, and about Michaelmas, through the abundance of rain that fell suddenly. (Brooks, p. xxxvii)

Ernest Schanzer interprets Titania's speech in terms of the Renaissance concepts of the macrocosm and microcosm: the idea that the pattern, proportions and hierarchy of the universe correspond to the pattern, proportions and hierarchy of humanity, such that levels of existence which are great and small, or cosmic and local, are linked together by structures of analogy. Hence disruption to the order of human society is equivalent to a breach of natural order, and vice versa. For Schanzer, then, Titania's speech is much more than just a topical allusion to bad weather; it is a description of 'disorder in the macrocosm' which, as so often in Shakespeare, accompanies and figures 'disorder in the body politic, here the state of fairydom' (1955, in Price, p. 72). We may take this beyond the immediate world of the play to draw connections with perceived disorder in the body politic of Elizabeth's England. In Ralegh's *The Ocean to Cynthia*, Elizabeth as moon-goddess has 'decline[d] her beams as discontented' (l. 251), with the result that

> All droops, all dies, all trodden under dust
> The person, place, and passages forgotten,
> The hardest steel eaten with softest rust,
> The firm and solid tree both rent and rotten.
>
> (ll. 253–6)

Elizabeth's personal mutability, identified with her femaleness, is seen as generating universal mutability and decay. It is unlikely that Shakespeare knew Ralegh's poem, which was not published or circulated, but, assuming that *The Ocean to Cynthia* does indeed belong to Ralegh's disgrace of 1592, it seems that both poem and play participate in a distinctive 1590s sense that the time is out of joint, and that this is attributable to the unbalanced exercise of female power (Berry, p. 146).

In *A Midsummer Night's Dream*, the subjugation to male rulers and spouses of both the Amazon Queen Hippolyta and the Fairy Queen Titania is shown as a more natural state of affairs than unbridled female autonomy. Both figures could be associated with Elizabeth I, but in ways which were tangential and necessarily evasive of direct negative implications. Elizabeth was frequently represented as a warrior-woman, especially in the wake of the Armada victory of 1588. However, images of her specifically as an Amazon were comparatively rare (Schleiner, pp. 163–80). This was because the Amazons had a mainly disreputable image in Elizabethan culture as unnaturally mannish creatures who dangerously inverted proper hierarchy and even murdered their own male offspring (Olson, 1957, in Price, pp. 79–80; Holland, pp. 49–51; Montrose, pp. 70–71). Edmund Spenser, for example,

in *The Faerie Queene*, his long epic poem of the 1590s in praise
of Elizabeth, is careful to distinguish between the virtuous
warrior-maiden Britomart, who is Elizabeth's mythical ancestor
and one of the poem's heroines, and the Amazon Queen
Radigund. Radigund is 'halfe like a man' (Spenser, *Faerie Queene*,
V. iv. 36. 8); she cruelly and unnaturally enslaves and emasculates
Britomart's lover, the knight Artegall (V. v. 20, 23–6), and her
'wandring fancie after lust did raunge' (V. v. 26. 8). Britomart, on
the other hand, having rescued Artegall, 'The liberty of women
did repeale' in the Amazon state, 'Which they had long usurpt'
(V. vii. 42. 5–6). It seems that Elizabeth can be appropriately
identified with a warrior-woman, but only with one who is clearly
not an Amazon and not a threat to conventional hierarchy.

Similarly the Fairy Queen herself both was and was not
associated with Elizabeth. It is true that Spenser's *Faerie Queene*
centres upon application of the title-role to Elizabeth, also named
as Gloriana; it thereby draws upon a strand of folk-tradition
which, unlike Shakespeare's play, regarded Fairyland as ruled by
a female monarch alone. The Fairy Queen also appeared at various
entertainments during royal progresses, including at Woodstock
in 1575, in East Anglia in 1578, and at Elvetham in 1591. However,
on these occasions she was a figure distinct from Elizabeth and
appeared to pay her homage (Holland, pp. 29–30). Like the
Amazon Queen, the Fairy Queen could have connotations which
would have made direct identification with Elizabeth troubling,
in this case those of sexuality and the occult. Indeed, Spenser's
Faerie Queene contains a vestige of this erotic aspect in Prince
Arthur's description of a dream he had of the fairy monarch when
he lay down to rest in a meadow:

> Most goodly glee and lovely blandishment
> She to me made, and bad me love her deare
> ....
> Was never hart so ravisht with delight,
> Ne living man like words did ever heare,
> As she to me delivered all that night;
> And at her parting said, she Queene of Faeries hight.
>
> (Spenser, *Faerie Queene*, I. ix. 14)

This Fairy Queen is very unlike the monumental, enthroned and
awesome figure of Gloriana who presides over the poem as a

whole; she draws instead on the folk-tradition of an encounter with a fairy mistress or elf-queen, which came to Spenser partly through Chaucer's *Tale of Sir Thopas*, and which endured later in Keats's poem 'La belle dame sans merci'. In this passage of *The Faerie Queene* she may well be a vestige of an early stage of composition before Spenser had decided to identify the Fairy Queen so closely with Elizabeth (Bennett, pp. 10–15).

I do not want to suggest, then, that Hippolyta or Titania are direct one-for-one representations of Elizabeth. Indeed, on the face of it, Elizabeth and Titania could not be more different. Elizabeth as imperial votaress is shown as ethereally impregnable to desire, whereas Titania is dominated by desire, first wilfully, in her attachment to the Indian prince, then humiliatingly and punitively, in her subjection to desire for an ass. In fact, Elizabeth is specifically exempted from sexuality by its displacement on to Titania: it is because the imperial votaress glides away immune to Cupid's arrow that it falls on the flower which enables Titania's enslavement to passion for Bottom. The penalties inflicted by the Elizabethan state for publications which incurred official displeasure could be brutal – in 1579, for instance, John Stubbs and William Page each had his right hand cut off for respectively writing and distributing a pamphlet opposing Elizabeth's current marriage negotiations.[2] Northrop Frye points to this as evidence that Titania could not possibly be a reference to Elizabeth: 'The consequences to Shakespeare's dramatic career if the Queen had believed that she was being publicly represented as having a love affair with a jackass are something we fortunately don't have to think about' (1986, in Bloom, pp. 120–21). However, such literal-mindedness seems inappropriate; instead, I would suggest that Patterson's idea of functional ambiguity is useful here. It is precisely because he has carefully distinguished Titania, and Hippolyta, from Elizabeth that Shakespeare is able to use them to explore the desirability of curtailing female power, an exploration which can itself, in safely indirect and encoded form, express the prevalent sense of unease with Elizabeth's female authority (Montrose, pp. 77–87).

Noel Purdon points out that Titania's degradation belongs to an ancient mythological tradition of the goddess or queen who is punished or diminished by being made to fall in love with a mortal or animal (1974, in Price, p. 177). Examples of this include Venus with Adonis (Ovid, X. 519–59, 681–739); Pasiphae, mother of the Minotaur, with a bull (Ovid, VIII. 131–7, 155–70, IX. 735–7); and Selene, a Greek name for the moon-goddess, with Endymion, a shepherd (Brewer, p. 391). *A Midsummer Night's Dream* is a play in which, emphatically, women are brought into line, and authority rests in the hands of fathers and husbands, dukes and kings. Even when Hermia and Helena finally get the husbands of their choice, it is not through their own powers but through the overruling of Hermia's father by an even higher patriarchal figure, Theseus – for whom the multiple wedding affirms his own conjugal possession of Hippolyta – and through the aid of another patriarchal figure, the Fairy King.

This is one of the many Shakespeare plays in which mothers, figures of female power within the familial structure, are curiously absent (Calderwood, pp. 2–7; Orgel; Adelman). Only two mothers are mentioned, and even then only to be marginalized and excluded: the mother of the changeling boy, Titania's Indian votaress, is dead, her life sacrificed for her boy-child (II. i. 135); Thisbe's mother is the part originally assigned to Starveling (I. ii. 53), but she is silently deleted and in Act V he appears instead as the Man in the Moon. Theseus's lecture to Hermia on filial disobedience in Act I figures conception itself as the quasi-divine act of a male progenitor alone, justifying absolute paternal authority:

> To you your father should be as a god,
> One that composed your beauties, yea, and one
> To whom you are but as a form in wax,
> By him imprinted, and within his power
> To leave the figure or disfigure it.

(I. i. 47–51)

Set against this view, though, and despite being safely placed in the past of the play, Titania's Indian votaress is a memorable figure of female fertility who inspires one of the richest passages in the text which cannot be easily ignored or forgotten. Titania tells how:

> Full often hath she gossiped by my side,
> And sat with me on Neptune's yellow sands,
> Marking th'embarkèd traders on the flood,

When we have laughed to see the sails conceive
And grow big-bellied with the wanton wind,
Which she with pretty and with swimming gait
Following, her womb then rich with my young squire,
Would imitate, and sail upon the land
To fetch me trifles, and return again
As from a voyage, rich with merchandise.

(II. i. 125–34)

The two women together mocked the 'big-bellied' sails of merchant ships as mere travesties of pregnancy, the votaress triumphantly flaunting the fruitfulness of her own womb. For G. Wilson Knight, this scene represents fairyland deriding the worldly preoccupations of humanity: 'as we watch Titania and her loved friend laughing at the "traders on the flood", imitating their "voyage" on the waters of life, we see fairyland laughing at storm-tossed mortality' (1932, in Price, p. 65). While the observation is valuable, I think we can go further to acknowledge the significance of gender here: Titania and the votaress are emphatically female, and the merchant ships are the vehicles of men's exploits and ventures. From the female viewpoint of the shore, the ships are inconsequential, their cargoes no more than 'trifles' equivalent to pretty flotsam (l. 133), their sails hollow, filled only with wind.

The most serious challenge to male authority in the play, the only truly equivalent force, is the uncontained fertile female sexuality represented by the Indian votaress, by Titania's league with her and intense maternal affection for her son, and then by Titania's passion for Bottom, which seems to take Oberon by surprise in its consuming intensity (IV. i. 45–60). At the same time Titania's voluptuously and magnificently pregnant votaress is a telling contrast to the chaste, watery, ethereal, imperial votaress described by Oberon in his account of his vision. The opposition highlights the fact that, although the imperial votaress is ostensibly revered for her chastity, this is at odds with the values of the rest of *A Midsummer Night's Dream*. Her perpetual and impregnable virginity renders her not only exceptional, mystical and quasi-divine, but also ghostly and almost deathly as she floats untouched across the scene, and she is identified with a moon which is chilly, insipid and dampening (II. i. 162). By contrast, the Indian votaress sails upon the land, and has a corresponding generous materiality

29

expressed in language not only of richness, abundance, and fullness, but also of merriment and pleasure.

The overall attitude of the play to perpetual virginity is also plainly expressed in the diction of enclosure and sterility in Theseus's lines to Hermia: as a nun she would be a 'barren sister', 'in shady cloister mewed', chanting hymns which were 'faint' to a moon which was 'cold' and 'fruitless' (I. i. 71–3). Rather than the static agelessness and timelessness of the imperial votaress, it is the 'quick bright things' of love and youth that the play invites its audience to enjoy (I. i. 149). Self-willed female desire is the most serious threat to the patriarchal order in the play and the source of its struggle and conflict; correspondingly, though, the happy outcome of the struggle, the 'concord of this discord' (V. i. 60), is the realignment of female sexuality with patriarchy, not its denial. The play prizes female sexuality which is directed into marriage and motherhood far more highly than sterile purity, and identifies it with the central values of fruitfulness, warmth and harmony as the four couples – not only the three Athenian pairs but also Oberon and Titania – move towards their final marital unions.

The direct reference to Elizabeth in the 'imperial vot'ress' passage has been read by some scholars as a compliment designed to be given in her presence in the play's audience. Linked with the *Dream*'s prominent nuptial theme, this has inspired further speculation that the play was originally composed as part of the celebrations of an aristocratic wedding which the Queen attended (Brooks, pp. liii–vii; Price, p. 17). However, in the contexts of both the ambivalent moon-imagery of the 1590s, and the attitude of the play as a whole towards absolute virginity, it becomes difficult to read the 'imperial vot'ress' passage as an unequivocal compliment to the Queen. As Louis Montrose puts it, the action of the play 'depends upon her absence, her exclusion' (p. 82). On other grounds of theatrical history and the nature of the play, some distinguished editors have provided strong arguments against the theory of performance at a royally attended aristocratic wedding (Wells, pp. 12–14; Holland, pp. 111–12). Whether delivered in Elizabeth's presence or not, though, both the 'imperial vot'ress' passage and the whole play could have served as a functionally ambiguous critique, whose negative implications were detectable but sufficiently veiled to evade open provocation. The principal interest of the play is not in iconic virginity, but in the progress and processes of love; and this will be the starting point of my next chapter.

3

Varieties of Love, Variations of Genre

Comedy is above all the drama of love; the conventional marker of a comic happy ending is at least one marriage, founded on the mutual desire of the two partners. In *A Midsummer Night's Dream*, we get marriage three times over – four if we count the reunion of Oberon and Titania – emphatically confirming that what we have witnessed is a comedy. It is a play where 'Jack shall have Jill,/ Naught shall go ill' (III. ii. 461–2), forming an outright contrast to another comedy by Shakespeare, *Love's Labour's Lost* (1594–5), composed not long before *A Midsummer Night's Dream*, in which the nuptials of another four couples are deferred and 'Our wooing doth not end like an old play:/ Jack hath not Gill' (V. ii. 874–5). Whereas in *Love's Labour's Lost* Shakespeare experiments with disruption of the conventional marriage-ending, the *Dream* ends precisely like an old play, and takes pleasure in convention and a sense of ritual.

Part of the sense of happiness at this play's ending is created by its participation in the relatively new ideology that marriage should be predominantly based on love. This is not the place to give a comprehensive history of attitudes to marriage, but in very general terms sixteenth- and seventeenth-century marriage-theory can be contrasted with that of the Middle Ages. In the earlier period, upper-class marriages were usually dynastic alliances rather than love-matches, and literary culture tended to locate passion outside marriage in what has been called 'courtly love' or '*fin amour*' (Cuddon, pp. 163–5), the devotion of a lover who self-deprecatingly styled himself as servant to his married mistress. Meanwhile, the Catholic Church emphatically advocated virginity, especially female virginity, as a higher state of virtue than matrimony. The Reformation brought shifts in these ideologies: marriage began to be prized as a means of preventing sexual irregularity and as a virtuous state in its own right; this in turn meant that marriage had to be what has been termed 'companionate', based on the contented monogamy of each partner; and this in turn meant that marriage needed to be based on mutual love (Haller and Haller; George and George). Enforced marriage was increasingly seen as a greater threat to the stability of family and society than clandestine marriage for love: thus a writer addressing 'the Gentlewomen and others of England' in 1593 asked, rhetorically, 'What is the cause of so many household breaches, divorcements, and continual discontentments, but unnatural disagreements by unmutual contracts?' (Bell, pp. 286–7).

A number of recent discussions of sixteenth- and seventeenth-century marriage have concluded that, although companionate marriage allowed some degrees of autonomy to women, these remained within restricted limits (Jardine, pp. 39–48; Neely, pp. 8–16). It created a social structure in which in theory '[m]arriage is an equal partnership', but in practice 'some partners are more equal than others' (Jardine, p. 48). As we have seen, in *A Midsummer Night's Dream* the final marriages are achieved through patriarchal means and on patriarchal terms; not only does Jack have Jill, but, as Puck goes on to sing, 'The man shall have his mare again,/ And all shall be well' (III. ii. 463–4). Nevertheless, the final scenes show a fortunate coincidence of free choice in love, including female choice, with the patriarchal social order. The strength of patriarchal matrimony is most powerfully reinforced if it is something to which the potentially wayward and wilful female *voluntarily* submits: if, like Rosalind in *As You Like It*, she willingly says 'To you I give myself, for I am yours' (V. iv. 116); or if, like Portia in *The Merchant of Venice*, she freely says 'Myself, and what is mine, to you and yours/ Is now converted' (II. ii. 166–7). We find the same joyful self-surrender in the *Dream*. Besides the resolution of Hermia's and Helena's affairs to their own satisfaction, Titania on waking warmly greets 'My Oberon' (IV. i. 75), and even Hippolyta, however we read her demeanour at the beginning of the play, begins Act V by affectionately addressing 'my Theseus' (V. i. 1).

However, in the course of *A Midsummer Night's Dream* other possible love-outcomes have been indicated, and, along with them, potential generic diversions away from comedy into tragedy. Various elements in the play give a sense that things could easily have turned out otherwise. The very first scene activates a sense of the obstacles to love and of conflicts from which a happy resolution will only be forged with difficulty. Theseus has won Hippolyta by violence and must now win her affection to validate the marriage, while Hermia is offered a blank choice between obedience, death, or enforced celibacy. Lysander reflects not only that 'The course of true love never did run smooth', but that even a fortunate love is subject to 'War, death, or sickness' such that 'The jaws of darkness do devour it up' (ll. 134–48).

Between this foreboding beginning and the fortunate ending, the middle part of the play oscillates between tragic and comic potentials, to both of which love is central. There is much emphasis upon the volatility and vulnerability of love, and a sense of how easily love can take the wrong track. Love is represented as in conflict with reason, and reason in turn is most often invoked when it is least in evidence, such as when Lysander, under the influence of the love-charm, abruptly transfers his affection to Helena:

> The will of man is by his reason swayed,
> And reason says you are the worthier maid.
> Things growing are not ripe until their season,
> So I, being young, till now ripe not to reason.
>
> (II. ii. 121–4)

There is acute irony in Lysander's portentous attribution to reason and maturity of what we know to be the sudden transformative effect of not only magical interference, but a mistaken intervention at that. Yet this accords with a wider recognition in the play of the arbitrariness of love, and its imperviousness to reason. There is no ostensible reason why Hermia should prefer Lysander to Demetrius; 'Demetrius is a worthy gentleman', and having her father's approval, 'must be held the worthier' (I. i. 52–55). The two suitors are virtually indistinguishable; on the other side, Lysander is 'as well derived' as Demetrius, 'As well possessed . . . My fortunes every way as fairly ranked' (I. i. 99–101). Here Shakespeare echoes Chaucer's *Knight's Tale*, a source to which he would return late in his career for *The Two Noble Kinsmen*. In Chaucer's narrative it is extremely difficult to detect reasons to prefer Palamon over Arcite or vice versa, and indeed the lady for whom they compete, Emelye, is made to transfer her affection rapidly and equably from one to the other. In *A Midsummer Night's Dream* Shakespeare squares Chaucer's isosceles triangle by adding another woman, and does make some superficial distinctions between the two females – Helena is taller and fairer, Hermia is more spirited – but even here, there is no *logical* reason to prefer one over another. The switches of affection among the four lovers are facilitated by a sense that the two men and two women concerned are effectively interchangeable; indeed it is a symptom of this that in writing or talking about the play it is all too easy to get their names scrambled.

Attempts in the play to justify love-choices on grounds of reason are thus exposed as specious. Instead, the source and strength of love is attributed not to the mind, but to the eye. Time and again eyes are referred to, either as the organs which receive the subjective impression of the beloved which provokes desire, or as the organs whose beauty is the object which inspires desire. Thus Hermia wishes that 'my father looked but with my eyes' (I. i. 56); Helena laments that Demetrius dotes on Hermia's eyes, which to him are like lodestars (I. i. 230, 242, 183); and both Lysander's and Demetrius's newfound passions for Helena lead them to eulogize her eyes (II. ii. 127, III. ii. 138–9). The eyes are both the subject and the object of desire, both active and passive, reflecting the scientific debate in the Renaissance as to whether sight was produced by beams from the eye striking the object, or by beams from the object imprinting an image on the eye (Donne, pp. 183–4, note on 'The Extasie', ll. 7–8). The eyes can therefore serve as a metonym for both desire and that which provokes desire.

At the same time, of course, sight is a faculty which can be impeded, and this in turn becomes a figure of the vulnerability of love. The darkness of night 'from the eye his function takes' (III. ii. 177), forcing the lovers to fall back on the even less reliable faculty of hearing, which Puck exploits to exacerbate their confusion and exhaustion (III. ii. 354–430). Most significantly, it is to the eye that the love-charm is applied; as Oberon says of Titania, 'with the juice of this I'll streak her eyes,/ And make her full of hateful fantasies' (II. i. 257–8). The eye, it is implied, is at once a lens which can be distorted, and an aperture through which the mind can be entered and altered. In relation to the rest of the play, Helena's lament that love is blind and 'looks not with the eyes, but with the mind' (I. i. 234–5) can only mean not so much that love is utterly incapable of sight, as that it is incapable of seeing accurately, and is an instrument of fantasy rather than reason.

Moreover, the shadowy tragic possibilities which are indicated in the course of the play include not only the wrong choice of love-partner, but choice of the wrong kind of love, including sex outside marriage, homoeroticism, and self-slaughter for love. Possibilities of pre-marital sex are suggested by the temporal setting of the play. By 'midsummer night', Shakespeare may mean to imply specifically Midsummer's Eve, the shortest night of the year, and the turning point at the middle of the summer. However, as in his inconsistent treatment of the passage of time between the first and last scenes of the play, and of the phases of the moon, he also operates a kind of double time-scheme in relation to the placing of the play within the annual calendar. At several points it is implied to be May Morning, the dawning of the first day of May, the festival of the beginning of summer. On stumbling across the sleeping lovers, Theseus suggests that 'No doubt they rose up early to observe/ The rite of May' (IV. i. 131–2). Other allusions keep the idea of May Day before us: Lysander arranges to meet Hermia in the wood 'Where I did meet thee once with Helena/ To do observance to a morn of May' (I. i. 166–7); and when the women trade insults about their relative heights, Hermia calls Helena a 'painted maypole' (III. ii. 296).

May Day was an ancient English rural festival which was marked by the young men and women of each parish going out into the woods to gather and bring back hawthorn branches (Barber, pp. 18–24, ch. 6). It could also be fairy-time: in Spenser's *The Shepheardes Calender* the King and Queen of the May are attended by 'A fayre flocke of Faeries' (Spenser, *Shorter Poems*, p. 89, l. 32). Since hawthorn blossom was known as may, the expression 'bringing in the May' meant bringing in both the month and the flowers, and indeed there are some incidental references to hawthorn in the play (I. i. 185, III. i. 4). The ritual thus denoted both the arrival of summer and the bringing of nature into the town, and in keeping with these themes it was also an occasion for courtship games. It is the subject of a poem by Robert Herrick (1591–1674), 'Corinna's going a Maying', in which he describes the bedecking of the town with 'white-thorn', such that 'each field turns a street; each street a park/ Made green, and trimm'd with trees'. He also emphasizes youth and love:

> There's not a budding Boy, or Girl, this day,
> But is got up, and gone to bring in May
>
> ....
>
> And some have wept, and woo'd, and plighted Troth,
> And chose their Priest.
>
> (Norbrook and Woudhuysen, pp. 455–7,
no. 206, ll. 30–31, 43–4, 49–50)

On the one hand, all of this makes May Morning an extremely apt and happy setting for a play about love leading to marriage. On the other hand, however, according to Phillip Stubbes, a Puritan who condemned the festival as pagan and immoral, 'I have heard it credibly reported . . . that of forty, three-score, or a hundred maids going to the wood over night, there have been scarcely the third part of them returned home again undefiled' (*The Anatomy of Abuses*, 1583, quoted in Barber, p. 22). Indeed, in Herrick's poem there is a strong sense that finding a priest to perform the proprieties of marriage is not the only end in view; there is sexual innuendo in the suggestion that there has been 'Many a jest told of the key's betraying/ This night, and locks picked' (ll. 55–6). Herrick's light-hearted jocularity is more like the tone of *A Midsummer Night's Dream* than is Stubbes's didactic moral opprobrium, but even so the play shares with Stubbes an anxiety that female virginity should be preserved until after marriage to the right man, and that May Morning, and/or Midsummer Night, could be a time not purely of merry-making but also of threat to this preservation. Demetrius warns the abjectly submissive Helena,

> You do impeach your modesty too much,
> To leave the city and commit yourself
> Into the hands of one that loves you not;
> To trust the opportunity of night,
> And the ill counsel of a desert place,
> With the rich worth of your virginity.
>
> (II. i. 214–19)

Hermia meets with ardent physical advances from Lysander and has to persuade him at some length to 'Lie further off, in human modesty' (II. ii. 63); Puck clearly expects that lovers in such circumstances would lie together, and that Lysander must be some 'lack-love' or 'kill-courtesy' (II. ii. 83). Both women are fortunate in their lovers' gracious restraint, but the danger that it might have been otherwise is partly indicated by the invocation of the erotically charged rite of May.

May Morning and Midsummer Eve blur into one in *A Midsummer Night's Dream* on the basis of their shared properties. May Morning, as the transition from spring to summer, and Midsummer Eve, as the transition from early to late summer, each serve as appropriate symbols of the turning point from youth to maturity, from maidenhood to wifehood, from adolescent virgin innocence to adult sexual knowledge. Angela Carter, a writer much influenced by this play as we shall see again later, coins a phrase for both dates as 'green hinges' of the year. In *Nights at the Circus*, Carter's winged heroine, Fevvers, goes through two pubescent rites of passage: her first attempt at flight, which takes place very early on Midsummer Morning; and her near-deflowerment by a Gothic villain, which happens on May Morning. Both occasions are described by Carter as 'the year's green hinge' (pp. 33, 78); like Shakespeare, she has it both ways, merging the two dates. Also as in *A Midsummer Night's Dream*, when the calendrical turning point coincides with readiness in a girl's life for her to become a woman, this coincidence confers an air of propitiousness and cosmic fitness upon a personal event, like Fevvers' first flight; but if that point of readiness has not been reached, the 'green hinge' is a potentially threatening time of forced submission to rapacious male sexuality.

The unsettling or even traumatic properties of the 'green hinge' from girlhood to womanhood are suggested in *A Midsummer Night's Dream* by moments of nostalgia for an earlier, more placid time of childhood. In the past, we are told, Hermia and Helena would enact their observance of the rites of May together, as girlhood companions. This was just one activity of what seemed an indissoluble female-female bond. As Helena reminds Hermia, they shared 'schooldays' friendship, childhood innocence', and, in a delightful simile,

> grew together,
> Like to a double cherry: seeming parted,
> But yet an union in partition,

Two lovely berries moulded on one stem
. . . with two seeming bodies but one heart.

(III. ii. 202–12)

In the Petrarchan poetry of the Elizabethan period the poet's mistress was frequently and conventionally praised for lips which were like cherries, an image which conveyed at once enticing rosy ripeness and untouched, unbitten wholeness. This is exactly the language which Demetrius uses when he awakes to see the newly beloved Helena – 'O, how ripe in show/ Thy lips, those kissing cherries, tempting grow!' (III. ii. 139–40) – and even Flute's Thisbe has cherry lips (V. i. 189). In Helena's speech to Hermia, the image of the cherry for the two girls has a similar mingled effect: it suggests at once an incipient ripeness to be plucked and an as yet unplucked, unspoilt completeness.

Of course the symmetry of a *double* cherry is also essential to Helena's representation of perfect friendship. David Marshall illuminatingly points out the relevance of the *Symposium* by the Greek philosopher Plato, an extremely important text for Renaissance philosophies of love (1982, in Bloom, pp. 105–6). In the *Symposium*, a fictional debate among different real speakers about the nature of love, the comic playwright Aristophanes constructs a semi-comic myth about the origins of human desire. He relates how each human being was originally a pair of our present bodies, with four arms, four legs and two sets of genitals; but when these creatures became over-ambitious and challenged the gods, they were punished by being split in two. The consequent sense of loss, says Aristophanes, is the source of human desire; when an individual encounters their missing half, they are consumed by a longing to rush into their arms and reunite their bodies. An original double creature which was half-male, half-female produces a heterosexual couple; all-male doubles produce homosexuals; and all-female doubles produce lesbians (Plato, pp. 59–65).

When Helena says that she and Hermia used to enjoy a unity 'As if our hands, our sides, voices, and minds/ Had been incorporate' (III. ii. 207–8) – that is, 'of one body' – there is a distinct echo of this fable. Aristophanes' story is a Fall-narrative: it identifies the desire for absolute union with a lover as a desire to return to paradisiacal pre-lapsarian happiness. This is what

Helena craves from Hermia, a return to an uncomplicated idyll of contented all-female innocence before the tricky business of relationships with men intervened. However, the signal that this would be a backward and fruitless step is also there in her language, when she reminds Hermia of their 'sisters' vows' (III. ii. 199). Here the echo is of Theseus's threat to Hermia of the nunnery, where she would 'live a barren sister all your life' (I. i. 72). His conclusion – 'earthlier happy is the rose distilled' (I. i. 76) – overshadows Helena's nostalgic plea for a regression to pre-adolescence, and makes clear that, whatever the temporary pains of the transition, the movement forwards into male-female union is one which must be made.

Valerie Traub finds in Helena's lines to Hermia an expression of female homoeroticism, and draws a parallel with the affection between Celia and Rosalind in *As You Like It*. There, Celia reminds her father that

> We still have slept together,
> Rose at an instant, learn'd, play'd, eat together,
> And whersoe'er we went, like Juno's swans,
> Still we went coupled and inseparable.

> (I. iii. 73–6)

The term 'homoeroticism' perhaps needs some clarification and some distinction from homosexuality. There is nothing in either play to suggest that Rosalind and Celia, or Helena and Hermia, have had a physically consummated sexual relationship. In this sense their attachments are asexual or pre-sexual. However, it would be an exaggeration to deny that there is any erotic element in each female couple's pubescent intimacy, which has clearly been both intense and based on attraction to one another's physical likeness. In this sense it is literally '*homo*-erotic' – that is, based on desire for sameness.

Traub is self-conscious about the fact that she is highlighting these passages in a deliberate quest to find examples of lesbian desire in Renaissance literature, and that unequivocal examples are elusive. She is also keenly aware that in both cases female homoeroticism is elegiacally placed in the past, such that its very function within the plays is that of something to be displaced and superseded by heterosexual desire. It is invoked as a valuable preliminary to heterosexual desire, a kind of training in affection and loyalty which softens a woman's heart and prepares her for 'real' love while safely preserving her physical purity; but at the same time it is shown as a false track, a dead end from which she must be turned aside and led towards her proper adult destiny of marriage.

A similar reading can be made of Titania's friendship with her Indian votaress. Her defiance of Oberon over the Indian prince is produced not solely by affection for the boy in his own right, but by her debt of affection for his mother. She intones ceremoniously, in the form of an incontrovertible vow,

> And for her sake do I rear up her boy;
> And for her sake I will not part with him.
>
> (II. i. 136–7)

As we have seen, she describes how she and the votaress indulged themselves in impudently mocking the masculine merchant ships as hollow travesties of pregnancy, and indeed how the two women revelled in the sensual spectacle of the votaress's richly pregnant female body. Yet all of this exclusive female-female affection and pleasure is also placed elegiacally in the past: 'she, being mortal, of that boy did die' (l. 135). Titania, too, has to be educated away from her loyalty to a female bond, whose time is over, to renewed loyalty to her marital bond. And Hippolyta is yet a further parallel case, in that she must be wooed away from another form of all-female community, the sisterhood of the Amazonian gynocracy, which has been defeated and dissolved by the masculine force of Theseus.

In general, same-sex love undermines the argument of comedy, and tends to be introduced in Shakespeare's plays only to be averted or superseded; other examples include Olivia's attraction to Viola in *Twelfth Night*, and, between men, the affection of Antonio for Sebastian in the same play, or that of another Antonio for Bassanio in *The Merchant of Venice*. For Helena and Hermia, heterosexual desire fractures their girlhood unity in a way which is temporarily antagonistic and even descends to vitriolic abuse. It causes Helena, only a few minutes after her 'double cherry' speech, to reverse her account of the past: 'O, when she is angry she is keen and shrewd./ She was a vixen when she went to school' (III. ii. 323–4). 'Shrewd' here means 'shrewish', like the uncontrollably violent and unruly Katherina in *The Taming of the*

Shrew. Ruth Nevo has pointed out that critics who say that all of the four Athenian lovers in *A Midsummer Night's Dream* change partners are not correct: the women never waver at all in their attachments to the men (1980, in Bloom, p. 58). What does go through a diametrical shift, however, is the women's affection for one another. This temporary estrangement dramatizes their conversion to more compelling heterosexual allegiances. Once the male-female couplings have been sorted out, female-female harmony can be restored too, but now as a secondary supportive substructure to the primary unity of marriage. The outcome is realignment in a new, doubled symmetry: 'Two of both kinds makes up four' (III. ii. 438). Just as the girls were once like a double cherry, now they are twinned again in a double wedding, a twinning to the power of two. This stress on symmetries, parallels and geometrical patterns, creating a sense of harmony and alignment, accentuates the happy feeling of the multiple marriage-ending. Premature defloration has been averted, regression to girlhood homoeroticism has been abandoned, and broken friendships have been mended on new terms.

This tidy patterning at the end of *A Midsummer Night's Dream* is a necessary counterpart to a coexistent sense that comic closure has been achieved by somewhat haphazard means, and more by accident than design. The final happy pairings of the young Athenians are largely attributable to the impetuosity of Theseus, who in Act IV, scene i abruptly overrules not only Egeus, but also his own earlier judgement and the law of Athens, which in Act I 'by no means we may extenuate' (i. 120). The only reason for his conversion seems to be that he is in a good mood and, in tune with the play, is anxious to move towards a happy ending to coincide with his own nuptials. He is at once the absolute authority in the mortal world of the play, and a rather capricious and arbitrary ruler, very like the Theseus of Chaucer's *Knight's Tale*, a work which, as we have seen, seems to have been in Shakespeare's mind as he composed the *Dream* (Fender, pp. 7, 12, 16–20, 25–6, 60; Brooks, pp. 129–34). The other chief agency which brings about the happy ending shares in this capriciousness, being the somewhat unreliable magic of Puck and Oberon. In fact, Demetrius must remain perpetually under the love-charm's spell, not cured by its antidote as are Lysander and Titania, in order for him to fall into position as Helena's willing husband. The troubling implications of this are only suppressed by the conventions of comic closure, by the sense of a neat and satisfying tying-up of ends, and by the general emphasis of the play on the limitations of reason, encouraging us to desist from rational objections. The closing mood of stability and order is thus built on somewhat unstable foundations; yet the sense that the ending is a happy one can be seen as precisely dependent upon this combination of stability and instability. The symmetries and parallels among the couples give a sense that the right ending has been achieved, while the sense that the means to achieve it were a matter of mere luck, of comedy fortuitously snatched from the jaws of tragedy, creates an air of relief and cause for celebration.

Besides the wrong kinds of love, another threat to comedy which constantly hovers over the play is that of death. Jan Kott attributes this to the fact that

> The *furor* of love always calls forth death as its only equal partner. Hermia says to Lysander: 'Either death or you I'll find immediately' (II. ii. 162); Lysander says of Helena: 'Whom I do love, and will do till my death' (III. ii. 167); Helena says of Demetrius: 'To die upon the hand I love so well' (II. i. 244), and again: ''Tis partly mine own fault,/ Which death, or absence soon shall remedy' (III. ii. 243–4). Even sleep 'With leaden legs and batty wings' is 'death-counterfeiting' (III. ii. 364–5). (Kott, 1981, in Bloom, p. 82.)

Harold Brooks has shown that one of Shakespeare's sources in the *Dream*, perhaps surprisingly, is Seneca, the Roman author of notoriously gory tragedies (pp. lii–lxiii, lxxxiv–lxxxv). There are particular echoes of Seneca's *Phaedra*, the story of the ill-fated son of Theseus and his Amazon bride, which Shakespeare would also have found in his Ovid (Calderwood, pp. 5, 58; Ovid, XV. 497–546). Hippolytus meets a brutal end when his libidinous stepmother, Phaedra, falsely accuses him of seducing her. As he flees in his chariot, his horses lose control and run wild, so that he is thrown to the ground, dragged along by his harness, and savagely torn to pieces:

> The ground was reddened with a trail of blood;
> His head was dashed from rock to rock, his hair
> Torn off by thorns, his handsome face despoiled
> By flinty stones.

His body is 'broken into pieces/ Hanging on every tree' (Seneca, pp. 141–2). In its relation to Seneca's story, *A Midsummer Night's Dream* is a comic 'prequel' to an excoriating tragedy of misplaced desire and doomed youth: the celebration of Theseus and Hippolyta's nuptials will have its outcome in Hippolytus's beautiful body violently torn to fragments on the shore. As Seneca puts it, 'That beauty,/ That form, to come to this!'

Shakespeare accentuates the link between Hippolytus and his Amazon mother by choosing to name Theseus's bride Hippolyta, the name given to her in Chaucer's *Knight's Tale*, rather than Antiope, the name given in Seneca and most other sources (Chaucer, p. 25, ll. 866–8). Another connection between the *Dream* and the tragedy of Hippolytus is the fact that Phaedra was the daughter of Pasiphae, whose union with a bull produced the Minotaur; thus the child of Theseus's union with Hippolyta will be annihilated by the child of a mother who engaged in a dark analogue to Titania's comic coupling with a beast. Beyond the opening lines of *A Midsummer Night's Dream*, in which Theseus incidentally expresses to his bride the innate antipathy between domineering stepdames and energetic young men, lies the future supplantation of Hippolyta by an evil stepmother who will tragically desire and destroy her youthful son.

Such peripheral threats of mortality, violence and tragedy can serve to intensify comedy, and there has long been recognition of the presence of darker elements in Shakespeare's plays. Often they can have a 'carpe diem' – 'seize the day' – effect, as in *Twelfth Night*, where Feste's remedy for the fact that 'Youth's a stuff will not endure' is to urge 'Then come kiss me, sweet and twenty' (II. iii. 51–2). There is a similar effect to Lysander's observation in Act I of the *Dream* that 'quick bright things come to confusion' (I. i. 149); if love is 'momentany [*sic*] as a sound,/ Swift as a shadow, short as any dream' (ll. 143–4) then its happiness must be fully and intensely enjoyed while it lasts, just as the audience are invited to enjoy the brief interlude of comic entertainment as a relief from the trials of daily life.

This speech by Lysander in the first scene of the play also catalogues the different varieties of doomed loves. In so doing, it invokes not only general griefs and dangers, but also a specific work of tragedy by Shakespeare himself. Lysander reflects on loves thwarted by difference of blood or choice of relatives, and Hermia replies that 'true lovers have been ever crossed' (I. i. 135,

139, 150). It is hard not to be reminded of Romeo and Juliet, that notable pair of 'star-cross'd lovers' (Prologue), and subjects of a play composed at around the same period in Shakespeare's career (1595–6). Mercutio mocks Romeo as stereotypically lovelorn in his tendency to cry 'Ay me!' and rhyme 'love' and 'dove' (II. i. 10); Lysander indulges in just such conventional coupleting when he falls in love with Helena (II. ii. 119–20; Fender, p. 42). Mercutio's fantastical Queen Mab speech (I. iv. 53–95) also anticipates the more extended exploration of fairyland in the *Dream*.

In addition, a further pair of tragically star-crossed lovers, Pyramus and Thisbe, actually make a lengthy appearance in *A Midsummer Night's Dream*. Like both Romeo and Juliet, and Lysander and Hermia, they are divided by the will of their parents and they make a secret nocturnal assignation to evade the prohibition on their love; like Romeo and Juliet, but, in the end, not Lysander and Hermia, a series of accidents results in their violent deaths. The inset play of the *Dream* thus reinforces the sense that the outer story of the Athenian lovers has tragic possibilities which have only narrowly been averted. At the same time, though, the story of Pyramus and Thisbe as performed by the mechanicals presents us with a tragic tale which has comic effect. The parallels with the vicissitudes of the Athenian lovers highlight ways in which tragedy and comedy alike depend upon mistaken identity, mishap, mistiming and misinterpretation.

The apparent oxymorons in the mechanicals' description of their play as a 'Most Lamentable Comedy' of 'very tragical mirth' (I. ii. 11, V. i. 57) are thus another joke with serious overtones: *A Midsummer Night's Dream* as a whole is a play in which Shakespeare actively explores the intersections of comedy and tragedy and the fluidity of generic boundaries. Jacques Derrida has argued that we might initially think of genre as a matter of definition and of essential qualities which cannot or at least should not be mixed (Derrida, p. 57). However, Derrida's general position as a deconstructionist is that there is no such thing as pure definition: each word in language, or each sign in any system of signification, takes on meaning through its difference from other words or signs, which it simultaneously excludes yet implicitly depends upon for contrast and distinction. Hence, for instance, the word 'masculinity' depends for its meaning upon its opposition to the word 'femininity'; 'femininity' is the other of 'masculinity', that which it excludes, but also that against which it defines its boundaries and without which it therefore cannot exist. 'Femininity' may even be that which 'masculinity' needs to exclude in order to conceal its own likeness to femininity, its own impurity (Eagleton, pp. 132–3). Similarly, for Derrida there is no such thing as pure genre, since any genre depends upon other genres for definition: what he calls 'the law of the law of genre' is 'precisely a principle of contamination, a law of impurity, a parasitical economy' (Derrida, p. 59). Thus a work which seems to belong predominantly to a particular generic category will always contain traces of other and opposite genres, by contrast with which the boundaries of the dominant genre are delineated. Much as a photograph is produced from a negative, or much as a silhouette is an image in black which would be formless without the white space which surrounds it, so comedy depends upon the implicit presence of tragedy, and vice versa.

In its allusions to wrong paths in love, to lurking threats of mortality, and to specific tragic analogues, *A Midsummer Night's Dream* offers particularly vivid illustration of this impurity and interdependence of genres. The next chapter will look further at the presence of alternatives in the play, at how they have enabled widely variant interpretations of its mood and meaning, and at how they have shaped different productions.

4

The Play on the Stage, on Screen, and in the Mind

Despite the tragic elements of *A Midsummer Night's Dream* which I have outlined, the dominant stage tradition over the centuries has been to present the play as a light, playful, good-humoured fantasy. For the seventeenth, eighteenth and nineteenth centuries it was essentially a pretty spectacle, lending itself to operatic and balletic decoration and peopled by hordes of delicate fairies in floaty white dresses (Plates 3 and 4; Halio, ch. 1). This tradition was inaugurated by Elkanah Settle and Henry Purcell's opera *The Fairy Queen* in 1692, which included 'a Chorus of *Fawns*, and *Naiads*, with *Woodmen*, and *Hay-makers* Dancers', not to mention a dance of six monkeys and 'a Grand Dance of 24 *Chineses*' (Halio, p. 15). Later, from 1833 on, the sense of a need for musical embellishment was provided by Mendelssohn's music, including the famous Wedding March (Halio, p. 22).

In continuing the light, bright idea of the play, Victorian productions felt it necessary to purify the text by excising any whiff of impropriety. In the nineteenth century the metaphors of the 'big-bellied' sails and 'wanton wind' in Titania's Indian votaress speech were omitted (II. i. 129); Hermia spoke of giving up her 'maiden heart' rather than her 'virgin patent' (I. i. 80); and at the end, instead of his shocking cry of 'Lovers, to bed', Theseus was made to say merely 'Lovers, away' (V. i. 355; Halio, p. 23). The Victorian tradition of representing the fairies as romantic creatures in white chiffon persisted until as late as Tyrone Guthrie's production at the Old Vic in 1937–8 (Plate 5) and Michael

Plate 3.
Hordes of balletic fairies in Act II, scene i of a production by Charles Kean, Princess's Theatre, 1858.

Plate 4.   The palace of Theseus in Act V of Charles Kean's 1858 production, with ninety fairies dancing.

Plate 5.

Tyrone Guthrie's production at the Old Vic, 1937 - 8, still in the balletic style.

Benthall's Royal Shakespeare Company production in 1949 (Foakes, pl. 6); as Lilian Baylis put it, 'I like my fairies gauzy' (Holland, pp. 25–6). An idea of the play as lightweight and innocent also endures in its continuing reputation as a play suitable for children.

However, the twentieth century also brought some experimental divergences from these conventions. Harley Granville Barker's[1] 1914 production, in which the fairies were metallic-clad orientals and the chief scenery was painted backdrops rather than elaborate sets, qualifies as the first modernist production (Holland, pl. 3; Foakes, pl. 4; Halio, pp. 31–6; Granville-Barker, pp. 33–9). In 1954 George Devine used harsh bird-of-prey type costumes for the fairies (Foakes, pl. 7); and in 1959 Peter Hall staged the play in the likeness of an amateur performance at an Elizabethan country house, with the fairies as mischievous nature-sprites (Halio, pp. 46–7).

It was inevitable, though, that sooner or later a play which presents itself as a dream would invite the application of Freudian ideas. Psychoanalysis provides a framework for investigating the subtexts of the play, and this is not necessarily anachronistic; medieval and Renaissance thought also embraced and explored the idea that dreams have hidden meanings (Holland, pp. 3–21). Michel de Montaigne, writing in the late sixteenth century, described how his own dreams were usually 'of fantastic and grotesque things, the products of thoughts that are amusing and absurd rather than melancholy', but nevertheless 'I believe it to be true that dreams are faithful interpreters of our inclinations' and that, as ancient authorities maintained, 'it is a wise precaution to draw from them prophetic instructions for the future' ('On Experience', p. 385).

Thus an idea that dreams operate on several levels has operated for many centuries. However, post-Freudian thought specifically provides a vocabulary for articulating subtexts which are sexual. Although he makes little overt reference to Freud, the Polish critic Jan Kott adopted this kind of approach in an epoch-making essay on *A Midsummer Night's Dream* in his hugely influential book *Shakespeare our Contemporary*, first translated into English in 1965. Kott asserted that 'The *Dream* is the most erotic of Shakespeare's plays' (p. 175). For him, the key to the play was the figure of the ass, and his bestial coupling with Titania: 'Since antiquity and up to the Renaissance the ass was credited with the strongest sexual potency and among all the quadrupeds is supposed to have the longest and hardest phallus' (pp. 182–3).

Not only does Kott find sex at the bottom of the *Dream*, but he also sees its representation of sex as extremely dark. He asserts that 'In no other tragedy or comedy of [Shakespeare's], except *Troilus and Cressida*, is the eroticism expressed so brutally' (p. 175), so invoking comparison with a Shakespearean tragicomedy which pustulates with images of venereal disease, lust and decadence; he also compares the *Dream* with grotesque and perverse images in drawings by Goya. The copulation of 'The slender, tender and lyrical Titania' and the priapic and hairy ass is at once monstrous and a release from repression:

> This is the lover she wanted and dreamed of; only she never wanted to admit it, even to herself. Sleep frees her from inhibitions. The monstrous ass is being raped by the poetic Titania . . . Of all the characters in the play Titania enters to the fullest extent the dark sphere of sex where there is no more beauty and ugliness; there is only infatuation and liberation (p. 183).

Kott's reading is more than just a trendy invention of the sexually liberated sixties. There is authority for it in the play, where Titania's sensual image for her embrace of Bottom has distinct coital connotations: 'the female ivy so/ Enrings the barky fingers of the elm' (IV. i. 42–3). The female vine entwining the male elm was a conventional Renaissance emblem for married love, but Shakespeare here gratuitously renders it more genital by introducing the metaphors of the vaginal ring and the phallic finger, strongly implying that Titania's amorous actions in the privacy of her bower go beyond mere cheek-pinching and ear-tickling (Calderwood, p. 62). Moreover, one of Shakespeare's sources, *The Golden Ass* by Lucius Apuleius (translated into English in 1566) was distinctly bawdy. In this satirical narrative the protagonist, Lucius, is transformed into an ass and enjoys several erotic encounters with women which are echoed in Titania's infatuation with Bottom. When Lucius is bedded by a 'noble and rich matron' of Corinth, he is concerned that he will hurt her with his huge phallus,

> But in the mean season she kissed me, and looked on me with burning eyes, saying, 'I hold thee, my cony, I hold thee, my nops, my sparrow',

and therewithall she eftsoons embraced my body round about, and had her pleasure with me (Holland, pp. 69–71).

Kott's essay was a major influence on Peter Brook's landmark Royal Shakespeare Company production of 1970. This *Dream*'s experimentalism included sparse, abstract staging, and the exploration of dramatic self-consciousness: the action took place in a white box around which the actors not currently on stage looked on from galleries. However, at least as controversial was the carrying off of Bottom to Titania's bower, during which he was borne on the shoulders of manly fairies, one of whom thrust a fist up between Bottom's legs to mime a massive phallus (Plate 7; Halio, pp. 63–4). The production had an orgiastic energy which was more celebratory and joyous than Kott's somewhat nightmarish vision of the play;[2] nevertheless, as in his account, sexuality was clearly very much to the fore, and this was accentuated by laying suggestive punning stress on words like 'weapons' and 'nuts' (Halio, pp. 64–5). For Brook, his production revealed the true story of the play as 'a man taking the wife whom he loves totally and having her fucked by the crudest sex machine he can find' (Calderwood, p. 60).

Robert Lepage's 1992 production at the Royal National Theatre, in which the cast wallowed in mud and water which represented sensuality, confusion, and the liquidity of experience, developed the tradition of Kott and Brook and, behind them, Freud and Jung (Halio, pp. 117–25). Other productions since Brook's, even if they have been less bold in other ways, have tended to sustain the suggestion that the pleasures which Titania takes with Bottom are distinctly physical. A further associated innovation by Brook has also become common practice, namely the casting of the same actors in the roles of Theseus and Oberon, Hippolyta and Titania. This is partly a practical expediency for keeping down the size of the cast, and may well replicate conditions in Shakespeare's theatre. However, it also creates a sense that the fairy action of the play is related to and a reflection of the action in the outer Athenian frame; that Oberon and Titania are the dream-personae of Theseus and Hippolyta through which the Athenian couple can enact their secret desires and work out their buried resentments. This reading of the play as having conscious and subconscious levels, and as exploring the release in the dream-world of emotions

Plate 6.
Titania (Sarah Kestelman) and her fairy attendants in Peter Brook's radical 1970 production at the Royal Shakespeare Theatre.

Plate 7.

Bottom (David Waller) is borne off to Titania's bower in Peter Brook's
1970 production.

which are repressed in waking life, clearly accords with Freudian methods of interpretation.

Bill Alexander, in his 1986 Royal Shakespeare Company production, worked a variation on the formula by doubling only Hippolyta and Titania, thus making the middle acts in effect 'Hippolyta's Dream', a 'fairy awayday', as Michael Coveney called it in his review, a fantasy through which she could reconcile herself to her marriage to Theseus (Halio, p. 79). More usually, though, both Theseus/Oberon and Hippolyta/Titania are doubled. This practice was followed in Ron Daniels's production of 1981, which opened in the month of Prince Charles's wedding to Lady Diana Spencer, and was apparently partly intended as the Royal Shakespeare Company's wedding gift to the royal couple. The reviewer Benedict Nightingale saw in the role-doubling the inopportune implication that 'Chuck might feel better about Di if he imagined her having sex with a prole with a donkey's head'. Jay Halio has commented more recently that the production seems less incongruous in retrospect, now that 'As things have turned out, nothing seems to have made the royal couple feel better about each other' (p. 77).

Different productions of *A Midsummer Night's Dream*, then, can illuminate the wide range of possible critical interpretations: it can be a lightweight family entertainment, or an orgiastic adult fantasy; a joyous celebration of love and marriage, or a near-tragedy haunted by infidelity and mortality. Productions can also, of course, experiment with transplanting the action to different settings and periods. A Western-style staging in 1958 apparently worked very well: the Athenians were dressed as cowboys, Hippolyta was a Native American princess, and Puck wore a Davy Crockett fur hat and sang his song to the tune of 'Home on the Range' (Halio, p. 44). At another extreme, a number of productions by East European directors in the 1970s and 1980s emphasized the theme of individual freedom set against official oppression, often using stark modern stagings to represent the violent antagonism between the forces of subversion and the forces of authority. In one such production a black Hippolyta with close-shaven hair entered the first scene flanked by guards and wearing military-style fatigues and dominatrix-style high-heeled boots (Halio, p. 133).

It is highly appropriate that *A Midsummer Night's Dream* should have inspired such a wide range of theatrical experimentation, since it is a play which directly urges us to think about dramatic performance and how it works. Act V, especially, engages in self-reflexive inquiry into the nature of dramatic artifice, in the performance of *Pyramus and Thisbe* before an on-stage audience. The Act begins with Theseus's memorable speech about imagination, which is at once a reflection on the lovers' accounts of the dream-like events of the previous night, and a kind of prologue to the mechanicals' play. Theseus is sceptical as to the reality of the lovers' experiences; they are

> More strange than true. I never may believe
> These antique fables, nor these fairy toys.
> Lovers and madmen have such seething brains,
> Such shaping fantasies, that apprehend
> More than cool reason ever comprehends.
> The lunatic, the lover, and the poet
> Are of imagination all compact.
> ....
> And as imagination bodies forth
> The forms of things unknown, the poet's pen
> Turns them to shapes, and gives to airy nothing
> A local habitation and a name.
> Such tricks hath strong imagination
> ....
> . . . in the night, imagining some fear,
> How easy is a bush supposed a bear!

> (V. i. 2–22)

The audience have superior knowledge over Theseus here, in that we have witnessed the nocturnal fairy adventures, and know that, within the terms of the play's fictional world of suspended disbelief, they 'actually' happened. Moreover, while the thrust of Theseus's argument is a denigration of imagination as unreliable and incredible, his words ironically take on an opposite effect, especially as regards the poet, who is made to sound impressively powerful in his ability to give shape to airy nothings (see Fender, pp. 49–50).

For the Elizabethans the word 'imagination' had a different sense from ours, at once more passive and more negative: ideally, it was an accurate medium of received impressions, but it could all too easily become a distorting medium and source of delusions

(Rossky, 1958, and Dent, 1964, in Price, pp. 93–7, 124–5). The latter is Theseus's primary sense, but, as Northrop Frye points out, in his words we can detect the term beginning to be converted into the more positive Romantic sense of an inspirational shaping power (1986, in Bloom, p. 130). His disparagement fails, and moreover is discreetly overruled by Hippolyta's thoughtful response (Girard, 1979, in Bloom, pp. 34–6):

> But all the story of the night told over,
> And all their minds transfigured so together,
> More witnesseth than fancy's images,
> And grows to something of great constancy;
> But howsoever, strange and admirable.
>
> (V. i. 23–7)

'Admirable' here means 'to be wondered at'; on the whole, this is a play which invites and enjoys wonder rather than reason.

Theseus's words can be usefully compared with a similar passage in a much later Shakespearean play, *The Tempest*. There, Prospero interrupts the performance of a masque by spirit-actors and reflects that:

> like the baseless fabric of this vision,
> The cloud-capp'd tow'rs, the gorgeous palaces,
> The solemn temples, the great globe itself,
> Yea, all which it inherit, shall dissolve,
> And like this insubstantial pageant faded
> Leave not a rack behind. We are such stuff
> As dreams are made on; and our little life
> Is rounded with a sleep.
>
> (IV. i. 150–58)

For Prospero – and perhaps for his creator, the older Shakespeare, now nearing the end of his career as a playwright – both the theatre (the Globe) and the world (the globe) are equally baseless fabrics. They are mere visions, insubstantial pageants, and 'such stuff as dreams are made on', and life has no more substance than a fiction. By contrast, for Theseus, and perhaps for the younger Shakespeare, poetry is a magical place where even the immaterial can be given a material existence. Theseus's later lines during the mechanicals' performance again anticipate Prospero's, and indicate a more positive conclusion whereby imagination can bestow grace on the insubstantial: 'The best in this kind are but shadows, and the worst are no worse if imagination amend them' (V. i. 210–11).

Prospero is a magician, and as such he devises and directs the masque of spirits; he also, in the course of the play, orchestrates various other visions, steers the course of events, and manipulates the actions of all the other characters. This has often led to his being regarded as a figure of the playwright within the play, through whom the nature and extent of the playwright's powers are explored. Alvin B. Kernan suggests a similar reading of Oberon, in his manipulation of the mortals and his creation of illusions: 'Oberon's magical forest is a perfect image of what a theatre might ideally be and do' (1979, in Bloom, p. 51). The framing of the forest by the Athenian first and last Acts enhances this sense of it as a stage within the outer stage of the whole play, adding an extra level of escapism to the theatrical experience. If we take the wood to stand for theatrical space, then Theseus's comments on the lovers' stories at the opening of Act V apply not only to fantasy in general, but specifically to drama and its illusionary powers.

In fact, drama, illusion and imagination, if we take fairyland to represent all these things, decisively have the last word, since, after Theseus's departure to bed with the (presumably sardonic) words ' 'tis almost fairy time' (V. i. 355), the fairies reappear to bless the house and close the play. Up to this point, the structure of the play presents Athens as the conscious, 'real' world framing the fantastic space of fairyland; but the return to the fairies for closure keeps open the question of which world has the greater reality, which is text and which subtext (Chesterton, 1904, in Price, p. 44; Kernan, 1979, in Bloom, p. 52). The influence of fairyland also remains to the fore in that, as already discussed (Ch. 3, above), one of the mortal characters, Demetrius, remains indefinitely under its spell, and indeed must remain in his enchanted state of desire for Helena in order for events on the mortal plane to turn out well.

This blurring of fantasy world and everyday world, the sustained partial incursion of the former into the latter, is implicitly expressed in Demetrius's bewilderment on waking: 'It seems to me/ That yet we sleep, we dream' (IV. i. 191–2). At the end of the play, this sense of suspension between two worlds is in turn communicated outward to the audience about to leave the theatre

(Brooks, p. cxlii). If the play has displeased us, we are requested to adopt Theseus's combination of literal-mindedness and gracious tolerance:

> Think but this, and all is mended:
> That you have but slumbered here,
> While these visions did appear;
> And this weak and idle theme,
> No more yielding but a dream,
> Gentles, do not reprehend.

(V. i. 415–20)

Yet this closing imprecation is spoken by Puck, an untrustworthy and ingenious trickster, and a denizen of the fairy world which has unsettlingly become the frame rather than the framed. This twist combines with the immediately preceding action of the play to challenge any rigid sense of the precedence of waking over dreams, of reason over imagination, or of reality over drama.

Again like Prospero, Oberon not only directs events but also, with Puck, observes them from the borders of the stage, placing before us within the drama the boundary between actors and audience (Brooks, p. c). This too prepares us for the more overt representation of an on-stage audience and a play-within-a-play in Act V. In both cases, the on-stage audience frames the inner action and mediates it to the audience in the theatre, performing reactions to which we in turn react. Peter Brook sees additional complexity in Act V, in the courtiers' efforts to display their aristocratic wit in their comments on *Pyramus and Thisbe*; for Brook, it is not merely that the courtiers look inwards as audience to the mechanicals and look outwards as performers to the wider auditorium, but their performance is also directed inwards, back into the play: 'They are playing Shakespeare to the mechanicals. They have turned the mechanicals, *in the middle of their own play,* into an audience. They are forcing the mechanicals to admire their courtly acting' (Halio, p. 66).

In one sense, though, Theseus and the mechanicals are very much in tune with one another: he scoffs at those who imagine a bush to be a bear, and the mechanicals, too, exercise extreme literal-mindedness, whereby the Wall and Moonshine must be given actual physical forms and nothing can be left to the imaginations of their audience. On the other hand, in other respects they place *too much* faith in the audience's imaginations, fearing that they will believe Snug to be a real lion unless reassured otherwise. On the whole, though, the failings – or, in comic terms, unintended triumphs – of their performance rest on over-literalism, on making airy nothings too solid, too material. There is an incongruity in Theseus's sympathetic pronouncement that 'The best in this kind are but shadows' (V. i. 210); Bottom and his friends seem far from shadowy or visionary, and instead are all too substantial.

Some critics of *A Midsummer Night's Dream* have seen Act V as a paradigm of the play as a whole, arguing that the unfortunate materializing tendencies of the mechanicals' performance are in fact an innate deficiency of theatre in general, and that the whole play of *A Midsummer Night's Dream* is too poetical and fantastical to be subjected to such inappropriate solidification. In 1817 William Hazlitt lamented that the play was generally used as 'an opportunity for processions, for the sound of trumpets and glittering of spears . . . a fluttering of urchins' painted wings . . . a . . . profusion of gauze clouds and airy spirits floating on them' (in Price, p. 32). This was partly a reflection of the current fashion for spectacular operatic-balletic style productions; but Hazlitt went on to dismiss all performance, arguing that *A Midsummer Night's Dream* was a work of poetry to be read, not performed.

> The *Midsummer Night's Dream*, when acted, is converted from a delightful fiction into a dull pantomime. All that is finest in the play is lost in the representation. The spectacle was grand: but the spirit was evaporated, the genius was fled. – Poetry and the stage do not agree well together . . . That which was merely an airy shape, a dream, a passing thought, immediately becomes an unmanageable reality. Where all is left to the imagination (as is the case in reading) every circumstance, near or remote, has an equal chance of being kept in mind, and tells according to the mixed impression of all that has been suggested. But the imagination cannot sufficiently qualify the actual impressions of the senses. Any offence given to the eye is not to be got rid of by explanation. Thus Bottom's head in the play is a fantastic illusion, produced by magic spells: on the stage it is an ass's head, and nothing more; certainly a very strange costume for a gentleman to appear in. Fancy cannot be embodied any more than a simile can be painted; and it is as idle to attempt it as to personate *Wall* or *Moonshine* . . . The boards of a theatre and the regions of fancy are not the same thing. (Price, pp. 32–3)

Another Romantic critic, Charles Lamb, had expressed very similar sentiments in 1811 (Marshall, 1982, in Bloom, p. 87). As the spectacular tradition of production persisted through the nineteenth century, so did this parallel critical tradition which saw the stage as the enemy of poetry; Henry Morley began his 1853 review of Samuel Phelps's production by pronouncing the *Dream* 'the most essentially unactable of all [Shakespeare's] plays' (Halio, p. 25).

Of course all these critics suppress the obvious fact that the *Dream* was originally written as a play to be performed. It is also an irony of Hazlitt's criticism that he seeks to substantiate his case by reference to the performance scene within the play. The mechanicals' embodiments of Wall and Moonshine certainly expose the potential inadequacy of dramatic representation. In *Henry V* the Chorus makes a humble apology for the limitations of the 'unworthy scaffold' and 'wooden O' of the theatre; in that play, however, this admission wins us over to apply our 'imaginary forces', and the Chorus's imprecation to us to 'Piece out our imperfections with your thoughts' has an inspirational effect (Act I, ll. 10, 13, 18, 23). In *A Midsummer Night's Dream*, by contrast, it seems impossible to give serious credence to Theseus's advice that by applying our imaginations we can make the performance good (V. i. 210–11). But the disastrous delivery of *Pyramus and Thisbe* is there for two reasons: first, of course, the actors' ineptness is a source of comic entertainment; and secondly, the contrast with the outer frame of the play accentuates what drama can achieve when it *is* skilfully composed and performed in such a way that it *can* work in concert with the audience's imaginations. We may not believe that Starveling is Moonshine, but we do not question the presence of moonlight in the rest of the play; we may not believe that Bottom is Pyramus, but we do, for the duration of the *Dream*, believe that the actor is Bottom. The text constantly invites us into the willing suspension of disbelief, including visual disbelief: whether the costume director has chosen an elaborate prop or minimalist make-up for Bottom's ass's head, we know that it is artificial, but a competent performance can use the magic space of drama created by the text so that we accept that the actor is temporarily Bottom, and Bottom is temporarily an ass.

One of the extremes of spectacular literalistic production was Herbert Beerbohm Tree's version of 1900 and 1911, in which the

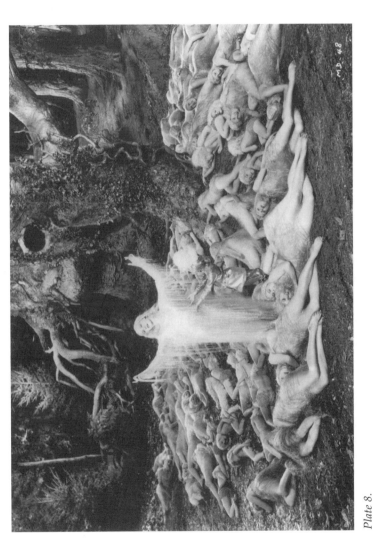

Plate 8. Titania and her fairies in Max Reinhardt and William Dieterle's 1935 film of *A Midsummer Night's Dream.*

set for the wood included 'a carpet of thyme and wild flowers, brakes and thickets full of blossom, and a background seen through the tall trees, of the pearly dawn or the deep hues of the night sky', and live rabbits scampered across the stage (Halio, pp. 30–31). At around the same period, the opportunities which the play offered for set-dressing and for special effects began to inspire exponents of the new medium of film; silent versions were made in America in 1909, and in France and Germany (Halio, p. 83). With the advent of 'talkies' it was again one of the first Shakespearean plays to be tackled, in Max Reinhardt and William Dieterle's version of 1935. Reinhardt and Dieterle took full advantage of the new technology at their disposal – hordes of fairies dance across the night sky on moonbeams, Bottom's face fades into the ass's head in the transformation scene – while also preserving for us on film what is essentially still a post-Victorian vision of the play, with vast elaborate sets for the wood and for Athens, with spangly, floaty white costumes for Titania and her throngs of fairy-followers (Plate 8), and with Mendelssohn providing a musical backdrop.

Angela Carter makes vivid use of allusion to the Reinhardt–Dieterle film in her last novel, *Wise Children*, 1991. The whole book draws on Shakespearean motifs, working a kind of fugue upon them; Carter is making the point that Shakespeare is not exclusive or élitist, but has for a long time been integral to popular culture, in the absorption of Shakespearean material into musicals, popular songs, colloquial idioms, and even street-names. Chapter 3 concerns the making of a 1930s Hollywood production of *A Midsummer Night's Dream* which is fictional, but obviously based upon the Reinhardt–Dieterle version. The set for the wood near Athens is sprayed with lavish silver paint, laden with huge artificial daisies, foxgloves and tree-trunks, draped with massive false suspended pearls representing dewdrops, and equipped with clockwork birds and a wind machine. Dora, Carter's narrator, who has been cast as a fairy, describes how the 'spotted snakes' and '[t]horny hedgehogs' of the lullaby for Titania (II. ii. 9–10) are all there,

> waiting in cages, snakes and hedgehogs, not to mention newts, worms, spiders, black beetles and snails, with snake handlers and hedgehog handlers ad lib at hand to keep them happy, waiting for their cue to

scatter this way and that across the set as soon as the fairy chorus started up.

It was all too literal for me. (p. 125)

Dora closely echoes Hazlitt in her dismay, but ironically she ends up celebrating the superior illusionism of the theatre:

What I missed most was illusion. That wood near Athens was too, too solid for me . . . there wasn't the merest whiff about of the kind of magic that comes when the theatre darkens, the bottom of the curtain glows, the punters settle down, you take a deep breath . . . none of the person-to-person magic we put together with spit and glue and willpower. This wood, this entire dream, in fact, was custom-made and hand-built, it left nothing to the imagination. (p. 125)

At the same time, just as the mechanicals' performance of *Pyramus and Thisbe* becomes an unintended comic masterpiece, so the Hollywood wood takes on a kind of unintended wonderfulness which is absurd, surreal and grotesque:

A giant mouse, saddled and bridled, trotted past. A bunny, in a wedding wreath and veil. Some dragonflies, in masks. Several enormous frogs. Dwarfs, giants, children, all mixed up together. (p. 129)

Decades later, in old age, Dora finds herself watching a screening of the film at an arty cinema where it is billed as a 'masterpiece of kitsch' (p. 111).

The fact is that authority for either a highly detailed, heavily laden materialistic production, or for a bare set, or solitary reading, which rely entirely upon the audience's imaginations to conjure up the accoutrements of the wood, can equally be found in the text. As Anne Barton has noted, characters in the play have a tendency

to stress the richness of their encompassing dramatic world by listing its components. Egeus is not content simply to state that Lysander has exchanged love-tokens with Hermia. He names them all: 'bracelets of thy hair, rings, gauds, conceits,/ Knacks, trifles, nosegays, sweetmeats' (I. i. 33–4). Almost all the characters are given to list-making. Oberon painstakingly itemizes every kind of wild beast that might conceivably wake Titania; Hermia and Lysander count all the obstacles that have ever threatened true love, while the fairies almost bury Bottom alive under a deluge of honey and butterflies, glow-worms, apricots and figs. (1974, in Bloom, p. 7)

Given this colourful enumeration of objects, combined with the presence of supernatural figures and transformations, it is easy to see why some directors of both theatre and film might feel prompted by the text to make lavish display of the visual effects which the technology of their medium affords; but equally, the words can be left to do their own work in inspiring purely mental visualization.

In directorial choices as to whether to go for an elaborate highly decorated set or for bare boards, and also in what we might call, to paraphrase Anne Barton, the 'thinginess' of the text, the wood as setting is obviously of paramount importance. This is the focus of my next and final chapter.

5

Nature and Supernature

Shakespeare vividly evokes the wood as a palpable physical space which is full of detail and movement: there are not merely snakes, but 'spotted snakes'; not merely hedgehogs, but '[t]horny hedgehogs'; not merely spiders, but '[w]eaving spiders' (II. ii. 9–10, 20). The intricate sensuous depiction of the wood produces some of the most lyrical passages of the play:

> I know a bank where the wild thyme blows,
> Where oxlips and the nodding violet grows,
> Quite overcanopied with luscious woodbine,
> With sweet musk-roses, and with eglantine.
>
> (II. i. 249–52)

Again, this tableau is full of animation – the thyme blows, the violet nods – and of verdant abundance, of 'luscious' plants which 'overcanopy' the scene.

The eglantine referred to in Titania's lullaby was the white dog-rose, often used as an emblem for Elizabeth I (see Ch. 2, above). The association of fairies with flowers can be traced back through both folklore and literary tradition (Latham, 1930, in Price, p. 61), but it had been given new impetus by its use in panegyric of the Queen. In the entertainment of the court on progress at Woodstock in 1575, a handmaid of the Fairy Queen presented Elizabeth and her ladies with 'many excellent and fine smelling nosegays made of all colours', and at Elvetham in 1591 the Fairy Queen told Elizabeth that she and her company 'every night in rings of painted flowers/ Turn round, and carol our Elisa's name' (Latham, 1930, in Price, p. 61). This fashion in courtly poetry was largely influenced by Spenser's 'Aprill' Eclogue in his *Shepheardes Calender* of 1579, which represented Elizabeth I as

'Elisa', a Queen of springtime who sits 'upon the grassie greene', and which urged her followers,

> Bring hether the Pincke and purple Cullambine,
>> With Gelliflowres:
> Bring Coronations, and Sops in wine,
>> worne of Paramoures.
> Strowe me the ground with Daffadowndillies,
> And Cowslips, and Kingcups, and loved Lillies.
>> (Spenser, *Shorter Poems*, pp. 75–6, ll. 136–41)

'Coronations' was a punning name for 'carnations', and 'sops in wine' were also flowers, a variety of clove pink used to flavour wine (Spenser, *Shorter Poems*, p. 76, l. 138n). This verdant tableau was the other side of the iconography of the Virgin Queen: as well as cold chastity and intactness, outside *A Midsummer Night's Dream* her virginity was also often associated with the unspoilt freshness and fertility of spring (Hackett, pp. 105–12, 176–80; Strong, pp. 147–51, 160). Again, I do not mean that Titania in her bower is an exact allegorical figure for Elizabeth I, but that royal panegyric provided floral motifs which were useful in elaborating a poetic image of feminine power. Spenser's catalogue of flowers offers incantatory and decorative pleasures which Shakespeare emulates in Oberon's lines on Titania's bower and elsewhere.

There are other verbal parallels between *A Midsummer Night's Dream* and Spenser's *Shepheardes Calender*, and with others of Spenser's works (Brooks, pp. xxxv, lxi–lxii). Dr Johnson saw Shakespeare's fairies as derived in part from Spenser's *Faerie Queene* (1773, in Price, p. 30); and indeed, in outlining the genealogy of Gloriana/The Fairy Queen/Elizabeth in his epic Spenser names her father as Oberon (*Faerie Queene*, II. x. 75. 8). Spenser was a poet both of fairyland and of pastoral, and in both roles evidently exercised an influence upon Shakespeare's composition of the *Dream*. Ovid's influence was also of particular force in this context: the *Dream*'s vivid depiction of the world of nature as a world full of supernatural presences emulates the richness of the *Metamorphoses*, in which the trees and flowers are peopled by spirits, the forest-creatures are anthropomorphic, and the landscape is teeming with vitality and activity.

At the same time, the flowers, trees and animals which people Shakespeare's wood not only draw on classical and courtly literature, but also vividly evoke the English countryside; just as his fairies, especially mischievous domestic spirits like Robin Goodfellow, were part of native rural tradition. According to Peter Holland, 'Robin belongs firmly and almost exclusively to a popular and folk-lore tradition'; he helped out with domestic tasks, especially by sweeping the house after the inhabitants had gone to bed, but if he felt himself unappreciated he would play tricks and pranks (pp. 37–9). Meanwhile, Titania, Oberon and their trains are at once lordly and exotic creatures 'Come from the farthest step of India', who mix with heroes of classical myth like Theseus and Hippolyta, and at the same time the presiding spirits of a world where the ploughman toils in the field, and turns for recreation to distinctively English rural sports like nine men's morris and mazes cut in turf (II. i. 69–80, 93–100). The play also draws on native rustic folklore in the way its fifth Act supplants the moon as classical, courtly, imperial goddess with the Man in the Moon, as played by Starveling, with his traditional accessories of thorn bush and dog (V. i. 253–4; Wilson, p. 15).

K. M. Briggs, an expert on folklore, has suggested that in the Elizabethan period there was an urban vogue for fairy literature, produced by a convergence between the courtly tradition of romance, which included supernatural figures, and the rise of non-aristocratic writers like Shakespeare who gave written form to the more humble hobgoblins of oral tradition (Fender, p. 28). Indeed, both Puck himself and the world of cowslips, acorn cups, hedgehogs and spiders which he inhabits must have had nostalgic and idyllic connotations for Shakespeare's urban audience. Just as Shakespeare himself was a native of Warwickshire, so many of his audience would have been born and raised outside London. At this time migration from the countryside into the capital in search of prosperity was taking place on such a scale that it has been estimated that by 1590 one in eight English people would spend part of their lives in London (Manley, p. 126). The London goldsmith Yellowhammer in Thomas Middleton's play *A Chaste Maid in Cheapside* (1613) fondly recalls his rural origins: 'The Yellowhammers in Oxfordshire,/ Near Abbington' are, he says, 'the best Yellowhammers, and truest bred: I came from thence myself, though now a citizen' (IV. i. 204–7). For many members of the theatre audience, then, the fairy-populated world of the wood would be the world of their youths and childhoods.

Helena's yearning for a return to a less complicated time of 'childhood innocence' (III. ii. 202) is paralleled in the play's recreation for its audience of the natural, folk-ritual world which they had left behind to pursue adult aspirations in the rapidly developing and competitive metropolis.

Angela Carter, again, in a short story called 'Overture and Incidental Music for *A Midsummer Night's Dream*' which explores and develops themes and motifs from the play, concurs in this sense of Shakespeare's wood as an Edenic prelapsarian space: 'The English wood offers us a glimpse of a green, unfallen world a little closer to Paradise than we are' (p. 69). She also regards this English wood as relatively tame compared with 'the dark, necromantic forest' of Germanic and Scandinavian fairytales (p. 67). The forest is a place of utter abandonment and loss of direction,

> But the wood is finite, a closure; you purposely mislay your way in the wood, for the sake of the pleasure of roving, the temporary confusion of direction is in the nature of a holiday from which you will come home refreshed, with your pockets full of nuts, your hands full of wildflowers and the cast feather of a bird in your cap. That forest is haunted; this wood is enchanted. (p. 68)

There are resonances here of the ritual of bringing home the May, the idea that after going out into the wood you bring a token of it home with you, symbolizing a revitalizing impregnation of civilization by nature.

In literary-generic terms, what we are clearly dealing with here is pastoral: a narrative in which characters leave their customary abode of civilization, whether the court or the city, and experience either voluntary or enforced exile in a natural space, where they learn a better understanding of themselves. The plot of pastoral closes with the characters bearing back to the court or the city the fruits of this new knowledge. Despite Carter's view of its relative tameness, the wood of the *Dream* is very much a pastoral space of estrangement and renewal, a place outside and beyond, variously referred to as 'a league without the town' (I. i. 165) and 'a mile without the town' (I. ii. 91). We should not forget that the town referred to is Athens, the ancient seat of reason. It is also the domain of Theseus, whom one strand of classical and medieval tradition represented as the archetypal man of reason who subdued revolted nature as personified by the Minotaur, the Centaurs, and the Amazons (Fender, p. 25). The wood's contrary irrational, or extra-rational, nature is perhaps best summed up in Demetrius's line, 'And here am I, and wood within this wood' (II. i. 192), punning on the Elizabethan sense of 'wood' to mean 'mad'. The wood, especially the wood by night in which the middle Acts of the play take place, is a topsy-turvy world of scrambled wits and distorted perceptions; this can be baffling, as it is for the four lovers, but it is also a place which allows the free exploration of possibilities which would be unavailable or unacceptable in the waking world.

The wood as a place of madness is also of course a place of comedy. Even Oberon, the authority who presides over this space, is not wholly in control, as his agent, Puck, accidentally mixes up the lovers and sows further confusion. Puck's attitude to the consequent 'fond [i.e. foolish] pageant' accentuates the fact that what is painful and frustrating for the characters can be farcical and entertaining for the onlookers, including us (III. ii. 114). For Puck, the result of his mistaken interference is 'sport', and 'those things do best please me/ That befall prepost'rously', that is, back to front (ll. 119–21). The inversions and absurdities which constitute comedy are all facilitated by the wood as a place beyond boundaries, a place of misrule.

The wood shares in the duality of the play; on the one hand a comic place of play and experiment, it is also a dark place with lurking threats and dangers. This is especially conveyed in the recurrent image of the snake or serpent. In Titania's bower, as described by Oberon, the snake is atypically female, sensual and protective: the bower is where she 'throws her enamelled skin,/ Weed wide enough to wrap a fairy in' (II. i. 255–6). However, shortly after this, in the fairies' lullaby, the first among the crawling and spiky things to be warded off are 'You spotted snakes with double tongue' (II. ii. 9). In general through the play these sinister connotations of the snake are predominant, its spottedness implying taintedness and impurity, and its double tongue suggesting duplicity, both of which are infective dangers to fallible humans. Demetrius, at the outset, in having abandoned Helena for Hermia, is a 'spotted and inconstant man' (I. i. 110); and when Hermia fears that Demetrius has murdered Lysander in the wood she declares that 'An adder did it, for with doubler tongue/ Than thine, thou serpent, never adder stung' (III. ii. 72–3). Hermia herself, however, becomes a serpent when Lysander spurns her: 'vile thing, let loose,/ Or I will shake thee from me like a serpent' (III. ii. 260–1). A serpent can be not only a faithless and venomous being but also a loathed creature which clings too tightly.

The snake has multiple mythical associations which lie behind these appearances. First and foremost there is the serpent of the Genesis story which brought about the Fall, a serpent which stands for deceit and temptation and which brought sexual knowledge and death into the world. There are also numerous snakes in Ovid's *Metamorphoses*: these include the monstrous satanic Python slain by the sun-god Apollo (I. 438–51); the serpent which bites Orpheus's bride Eurydice immediately after their wedding, causing her to be carried away to the underworld and parted from her grief-stricken husband (X. 8–10); and the nymph Salmacis who is besotted with the beautiful but unresponsive boy Hermaphroditus and twines herself around him like a serpent as he swims (IV. 361–3). The multiple connotations of the snake in Ovid's classical narratives are not unlike its resonances in Judaeo-Christian iconography: in Ovid too it stands for forces of darkness and for death and sexuality.

The prelapsarian space of the wood in the *Dream* is persistently haunted by this lapsarian creature. Perhaps its most vivid appearance is when Hermia, unknowingly abandoned by Lysander in her sleep, cries out,

> Help me, Lysander, help me! Do thy best
> To pluck this crawling serpent from my breast!
> Ay me, for pity. What a dream was here?
> Lysander, look how I do quake with fear.
> Methought a serpent ate my heart away,
> And you sat smiling at his cruel prey.

(II. ii. 151–6)

Although at many points in the *Dream* we see sleepers on stage, this is in fact the only literal dream, as opposed to dream-like experience, in the whole play (Holland, pp. 108, 4). Snakes were regarded as highly significant symbols in the dream-theory of the Middle Ages and Renaissance (Holland, pp. 7–9), and Hermia's serpent is imbued with a multi-layered suggestiveness by its context in the play. On the one hand it looks back to Hermia's last waking dialogue with Lysander, in which he pleaded to be allowed to sleep with her:

> my heart unto yours is knit,
> So that but one heart we can make of it.
> Two bosoms interchainèd with an oath;
> So, then, two bosoms and a single troth.
> Then by your side no bed-room me deny;
> For lying so, Hermia, I do not lie.

(II. ii. 53–8)

Hermia modestly diverts his desire and persuades him to 'Lie further off' (II. ii. 63). Although the exchange is superficially amiable, her anxieties are suggested in her ostensible compliment 'Lysander riddles very prettily' (II. ii. 59); implicitly she fears that Lysander may be a smooth-tongued deceiver. The snake in her dream, then, can be interpreted as a phallic figure, giving form to her repressed fear of sexuality, and specifically her fear that Lysander's satisfaction of his physical designs upon her may reveal the shallowness of his professed love and bring it to an abrupt end.

On the other hand, the dream is also prophetic, warning Hermia of Lysander's actual desertion of her which has taken place while she was sleeping. In this case, the serpent stands for the duplicity which, unknown to her, has already taken hold of her lover. Lysander smiles as his conversion devours her heart with grief because his affection for her has abruptly evaporated. In this sense Hermia's waking scene is full of pathos created by multiple dramatic irony: the audience knows what she does not, that Lysander has left her; the dream tries to warn her of what has happened, but she remains distressed but uncomprehending; and her whole panicky waking speech is addressed to a Lysander whom she does not realize is no longer there, so that her cries for help fall into a void.

In all these ways, the snake stands for the shadowy tragic threats which haunt the periphery of the action and which are overcome or deflected to produce comedy. The multiple references to snakes in the play render them at once highly symbolic creatures, denizens of the imagination, and precisely visualized real natural creatures, denizens of a real natural wood; just as the wood itself is at once a recognizable English landscape and a symbolic space peopled by potent invisible spirits.

The infusion of nature with the supernatural is one of the most powerful effects of *A Midsummer Night's Dream*, and is something which Shakespeare took up again in *The Tempest*. There Ariel sings to his spirit-cohorts:

> Come unto these yellow sands,
>   And then take hands:
> Curtsied when you have, and kiss'd
>   The wild waves whist:
> Foot it featly here and there.
>
> (I. ii. 375–9)

There is an echo here of 'Neptune's yellow sands' where Titania enjoyed her revels with her Indian votaress (II. i. 126). Later Prospero invokes

> Ye elves of hills, brooks, standing lakes, and groves,
> And ye that on the sands with printless foot
> Do chase the ebbing Neptune, and do fly him
> When he comes back; you demi-puppets that
> By moonshine do the green sour ringlets make.
>
> (V. i. 33–7)

In both plays, the natural world is vividly depicted as full of burgeoning and dancing vitality, and swarming with fleet-footed spirits, disembodied voices, and baffling illusions.

This was an aspect of Shakespeare's work which was especially fertile in its influence on later writers. A couple of prominent examples, whom I shall discuss briefly here, were John Milton and John Keats. Milton responded to Shakespeare as 'sweetest Shakespeare fancy's child' who '[w]arble[s] his native wood-notes wild' ('L'Allegro', 1632, p. 138, ll. 134–5). Clearly for Milton Shakespeare's 'fancy' – that is, his imaginative inventiveness – and his 'wood-notes' – his grounding in nature – were qualities which were interlinked. It seems very likely that *A Midsummer Night's Dream* was one of the works which Milton had in mind here, and his words certainly shaped the view of the play for subsequent generations; J. O. Halliwell-Phillipps, for instance, referred to the 'native woodnotes wild' of the *Dream* in an essay on the play in 1879 (Price, p. 40). Among Milton's own work,

Comus (1634) clearly shows the influence of the supernaturalized nature of the *Dream* and *The Tempest*:

> The sounds, and seas with all their finny drove
> Now to the moon in wavering morris move,
> And on the tawny sands and shelves,
> Trip the pert fairies and the dapper elves;
> By dimpled brook, and fountain-brim,
> The wood-nymphs decked with daisies trim,
> Their merry wakes and pastimes keep;
> What hath night to do with sleep?

(p. 182, ll. 115–22)

The combination here of detail and movement, abundance and delicacy, is unmistakably indebted to the fairy world of *A Midsummer Night's Dream*. Milton also picks up and in fact more intensely polarizes the moral ambivalence of Shakespeare's fairyland. Shakespeare's fairies can be malevolent as well as benign: Puck takes wicked pleasure in spilling ale and snatching away stools (II. i. 47–55), discord among the fairies has disastrous meteorological consequences, and arbitrary whims or mistakes by invisible fairy spirits can divert human intentions into potentially tragic courses. The spirit world of Milton's poem, so beautifully evoked in the passage quoted above, is the realm of the enchanter Comus, son of Circe, a purveyor of evil temptations, and both he and his world are alluring only in proportion as their sensuous attractions must be resisted by the virtuous.

The version of Shakespeare as combining 'fancy' with 'native wood-notes' also bore literary progeny among the Romantic poets, especially John Keats. For him, 'The poetry of Shakespeare is generally free as is the wind – a perfect thing of the elements, winged and sweetly coloured', a simultaneously natural and ethereal phenomenon (Spurgeon, p. 6). In Keats's own copy of Shakespeare's works he added marginal annotations, and these are most frequent in *The Tempest* and *A Midsummer Night's Dream*. Not surprisingly, he was particularly taken with passages in the *Dream* like the fairies' songs, with their sensuous natural observation; and Theseus's speech on the imagination, which readily lends itself to appropriation for the Romantic ideology of imagination as a god-like power of creative genius (Spurgeon, pp. 87–104). In Keats's own work, recollections of Shakespeare's play are especially prominent in *Endymion* (1818), where, for instance, Shakespeare's fairies' meeting-places, 'in grove, or green,/ By fountain clear, or spangled starlight sheen' (II. i. 27–8), are recalled by the 'Echoing grottos, full of tumbling waves/ And moonlight . . . all the mazy world/ Of silvery enchantment' (I. 459–61); and where are found 'shaping visions all about my sight/ Of colours, wings, and bursts of spangly light' (I. 568–9; see also Spurgeon, pp. 14–16, 19–20, 29–30, 51–2, 62–5). The closing lines of Keats's 'Ode to a Nightingale' (1819) also suggest a reminiscence of the musings of Shakespeare's awakening Athenian lovers:

> Was it a vision, or a waking dream?
> Fled is that music: – do I wake or sleep?
>
> ('Ode to a Nightingale', ll. 79–80)

> Are you sure
> That we are awake? It seems to me
> That yet we sleep, we dream.
>
> (*A Midsummer Night's Dream*, in
> *The Riverside Shakespeare*, IV. i. 191–3)[1]

The sense here of a desire to linger in the trance-like languor of sleep and the fantastic visions of the dream-world is appropriated and accentuated by Keats's Romantic sensibility.

The wood outside Athens, then, became a space of imaginative possibility not just for Shakespeare's characters, not just for theatre-audiences and readers whom the text invites actively to engage their faculties of visualization and fantasy, but also for later creative writers. This artistic fertility endures up to the present day, as the *Dream* continues to inspire contemporary writers like Angela Carter, as we have seen. The play also has a lineage in music, from Purcell through Mendelssohn to Benjamin Britten's twentieth-century opera; and in film and musical, from Ingmar Bergman's *Smiles of a Summer Night* (1955) to Stephen Sondheim's *A Little Night Music* (filmed 1977) and Woody Allen's *A Midsummer Night's Sex Comedy* (1982). Meanwhile, *A Midsummer Night's Dream* itself continues to be one of the most frequently staged Shakespeare plays and one of the most reliable box-office earners for the Royal Shakespeare Company and others. As I write, a film of Adrian Noble's 1994 RSC production is in process.

This study has tried to sketch some of the places which the play comes from, including literary sources like Ovid and Golding, the contemporary cultural context of the late years of a female monarch's reign, literary conventions of genre, and popular traditions of festival and folklore. However, it is also a play whose vitality extends forwards dynamically into the present, and continues to shape itself into new metamorphoses. Just as the play is full of different kinds of change, so it offers itself to be changed and made anew as it is encountered by each generation.

Notes

CHAPTER 2. THE PLAY IN ITS TIME: FEMALE POWER

1 A rural game played on a marked area of turf.
2 I am indebted to Henry Woudhuysen for the information that it was probably not Hugh Singleton, the printer of the pamphlet, who lost his hand with Stubbs, but William Page, who had sent copies to the West Country.

CHAPTER 4. THE PLAY ON THE STAGE, ON SCREEN, AND IN THE MIND

1 He did not hyphenate his name until after 1918 (Granville-Barker, p. 8, n. 1).
2 I am indebted to Sarah Wintle for an eye-witness account.

CHAPTER 5. NATURE AND SUPERNATURE

1 I quote here from the *Riverside*, rather than the Oxford edition, because the former but not the latter includes the words 'Are you sure/ That we are awake?', which are found in the Quarto but not the Folio.

Select Bibliography and References

EDITIONS OF *A MIDSUMMER NIGHT'S DREAM*

Andrews, John F., The Everyman Shakespeare (London: J.M. Dent, 1993). Introductory material very brief. Restores some of the punctuation and spelling of the earliest editions, though for rather superficial reasons. The least useful of the editions listed here.

Barton, Anne, Introduction to *A Midsummer Night's Dream*, in *The Riverside Shakespeare*, ed. G. Blakemore Evans (Boston: Houghton Mifflin, 1974), pp. 217–21. Short but richly observant and suggestive essay, also available in Bloom, below.

Brooks, Harold F., The Arden Shakespeare (1979; London and New York: Routledge, 1988). Comprehensive and scholarly account of sources, followed by equally thorough account of the play. Useful compendium of source materials in appendix.

Foakes, R. A., The New Cambridge Shakespeare (Cambridge: Cambridge University Press, 1984). Relates the play's stage history to polarized interpretations of it as either merrily innocent or darkly erotic. Good illustrations and informative account of literary sources.

Holland, Peter, World's Classics (1994; Oxford and New York: Oxford University Press, 1995). Detailed and interesting discussion of Shakespeare's responses to sources and contexts. Especially useful on medieval and Renaissance dream-theory.

Wells, Stanley, The New Penguin Shakespeare (Harmondsworth: Penguin, 1967). As accomplished and reliable as everything Wells writes on Shakespeare, but inevitably limited by its date.

CRITICAL WORKS

Barber, C. L., *Shakespeare's Festive Comedy: a study of dramatic form and its relation to social custom* (1959; Princeton, NJ: Princeton University Press, pb. edn, 1972), pp. 18–24, 119–62. Invaluable account of the play in relation to traditional May and Midsummer festivals.

Bloom, Harold (ed.), *William Shakespeare's 'A Midsummer Night's Dream'*, Modern Critical Interpretations series (New York and Philadelphia: Chelsea House, 1987). Wide-ranging collection of illuminating essays, including Anne Barton, Jan Kott, and Northrop Frye.

Calderwood, James L., *A Midsummer Night's Dream*, Harvester New Critical Introductions to Shakespeare series (Hemel Hempstead: Harvester Wheatsheaf, 1992). A psychoanalytical reading. Concentrates on relationships, the gaze, and liminality; less on dreams than one might expect.

Fender, Stephen, *A Midsummer Night's Dream*, Studies in English Literature series, no. 35 (London: Edward Arnold, 1968). Centres on the figure of Theseus to consider truth and rationality and their ambiguities in the play. Insightful analysis of language.

Halio, Jay L., *A Midsummer Night's Dream*, Shakespeare in Performance series (Manchester and New York: Manchester University Press, 1994). Survey of pre-1900 stage history followed by detailed accounts of key twentieth-century stagings, especially those of Brook, Reinhardt and Lepage. Fewer illustrations than one might expect.

Kott, Jan, 'Titania and the Ass's Head', in *Shakespeare our Contemporary*, trans. Boleslaw Taborski (1965; London: Routledge, 1988), pp. 171–90. Influential view of the play as concerned with dark, bestial, grotesque sexuality.

Montrose, Louis A., '*A Midsummer Night's Dream* and the Shaping Fantasies of Elizabethan Culture: Gender, Power, Form', in *Rewriting the Renaissance: the discourses of sexual difference in early modern Europe*, eds Margaret W. Ferguson, Maureen Quilligan, and Nancy J. Vickers (Chicago and London: University of Chicago Press, 1986), pp. 65–87. Ground-breaking new historicist account of the play in relation to the 'cult' of Elizabeth I.

Price, Antony (ed.), *A Midsummer Night's Dream*, Casebook series (Houndmills: Macmillan, 1983). Gives most coverage to critical studies 1930–74, but also includes some useful earlier critical responses and some material about twentieth-century productions. Prefers mythological and character-based readings over those which use political or historical contexts.

Wilson, Richard, 'The Kindly Ones: The Death of the Author in Shakespearean Athens', in *Literature and Censorship*, ed. Nigel Smith, *Essays and Studies* 1993, pp. 1–24. New historicist reading in the context of 1590s unrest and the vulnerability of royal authority.

OTHER REFERENCES

Adelman, Janet, *Suffocating Mothers: fantasies of maternal origin in Shakespeare's plays, 'Hamlet' to 'The Tempest'* (London and New York: Routledge, 1992).

Bell, Ilona, *Passion Lends Them Power: the poetry, politics and practice of Elizabethan courtship* (Cambridge: Cambridge University Press, forthcoming).

Bennett, Josephine Waters, *The Evolution of 'The Faerie Queene'* (Chicago: University of Chicago Press, 1942).

Berry, Philippa, *Of Chastity and Power: Elizabethan literature and the unmarried Queen* (London and New York: Harvester, 1989).

Brewer, *Brewer's Dictionary of Phrase and Fable*, by Ivor H. Evans (1959; London: Cassell, 1981).

Carter, Angela, *Nights at the Circus* (1984; London: Picador, 1985).

——'Overture and Incidental Music for *A Midsummer Night's Dream*', in *Black Venus* (1985; London: Picador, 1986), pp. 63–76.

——*Wise Children* (1991; London: Vintage, 1992).

Chapman, George, *The Poems of George Chapman*, ed. Phyllis Brooks Bartlett (New York: Modern Language Association, 1941).

Chaucer, Geoffrey, *The Complete Works of Geoffrey Chaucer*, ed. F. N. Robinson, 2nd edn (1957; Oxford: Oxford University Press, 1974).

Cuddon, J. A., *A Dictionary of Literary Terms*, rev. edn (1979; Harmondsworth: Penguin, 1982).

Derrida, Jacques, 'The law of genre', trans. Avital Ronell, *Critical Inquiry*, 7:1 (Autumn 1980), *On Narrative*, ed. W. J. T. Mitchell, pp. 55–81.

DNB (*Dictionary of National Biography*), eds Leslie Stephen and Sidney Lee, 63 vols (London: Smith, Elder, 1885–1900).

Donne, John, *The Elegies and the Songs and Sonnets*, ed. Helen Gardner (Oxford: Clarendon, 1965).

Eagleton, Terry, *Literary Theory: an introduction* (Oxford: Blackwell, 1983).

Eliot, T. S., *The Waste Land and other poems* (1940; London: Faber, 1972).

Fellowes, E. H. (ed.), *English Madrigal Verse 1588–1632*, 3rd edn, eds F. W. Sternfeld and D. Greer (Oxford: Oxford University Press, 1967).

George, C. and K. George, *The Protestant Mind of the English Reformation* (Princeton, NJ: Princeton University Press, 1961).

Granville-Barker, Harley, 'Preface to *A Midsummer Night's Dream*', in *More Prefaces to Shakespeare*, ed. Edward M. Moore (Princeton, NJ: Princeton University Press, 1974), pp. 94–134.

Hackett, Helen, *Virgin Mother, Maiden Queen: Elizabeth I and the cult of the Virgin Mary* (Houndmills: Macmillan, 1995).

Haigh, Christopher (ed.), *The Reign of Elizabeth I* (Houndmills: Macmillan, 1984).

Haller, W. and M. Haller, 'The Puritan Art of Love', *Huntington Library Quarterly* 5 (1941–2), pp. 235–72.

Hurault, André, Sieur de Maisse, *Journal*, trans. and eds G. B. Harrison and R. A. Jones (London: Nonesuch, 1931).

Jardine, Lisa, *Still Harping on Daughters: women and drama in the age of Shakespeare*, 2nd edn (1983; Hemel Hempstead: Harvester Wheatsheaf, 1989).

Manley, Lawrence, *Literature and Culture in Early Modern London* (Cambridge: Cambridge University Press, 1995).

May, Steven W. (ed.), *The Elizabethan Courtier Poets* (Columbia, Mo: University of Missouri Press, 1991).

Middleton, Thomas, *A Chaste Maid in Cheapside*, ed. Alan Brissenden, New Mermaids (1968; London: A. and C. Black, 1988).

Milton, John, *Complete Shorter Poems*, ed. John Carey (1968; London: Longman, 1971).

Montaigne, Michel de, *Essays*, trans. J. M. Cohen (Harmondsworth: Penguin, 1958).

Neely, Carol Thomas, *Broken Nuptials in Shakespeare's Plays* (New Haven and London: Yale University Press, 1985).

Nichols, John (ed.), *The Progresses and Public Processions of Queen Elizabeth*, 3 vols (London: Society of Antiquaries, 1823).

Norbrook, David, and H. R. Woudhuysen (eds), *The Penguin Book of Renaissance Verse 1509–1659* (London: Allen Lane–Penguin, 1992).

OED (Oxford English Dictionary), *A New English Dictionary on Historical Principles*, ed. James A. Murray, 10 vols (Oxford: Clarendon, 1901).

Orgel, Stephen, 'Prospero's Wife', in *Rewriting the Renaissance: the discourses of sexual difference in early modern Europe*, eds Margaret W. Ferguson, Maureen Quilligan, and Nancy J. Vickers (Chicago and London: University of Chicago Press, 1986), pp. 50–64.

Ovid, *Metamorphoses*, Books I–VIII, trans. Frank Justus Miller, rev. G. P. Gould, Loeb Classical Library (1916; Cambridge, Mass. and London: Harvard University Press, 1977).

——*Metamorphoses*, Books IX–XV, trans. Frank Justus Miller, Loeb Classical Library (London: William Heinemann, 1916).

Patterson, Annabel, *Censorship and Interpretation: the conditions of writing and reading in early modern England* (Madison: University of Wisconsin Press, 1984).

Peele, George, *The Life and Works of George Peele*, gen. ed. Charles Tyler Prouty, 3 vols (New Haven: Yale University Press, 1952, 1961, 1970).

Plato, *The Symposium*, trans. Walter Hamilton (Harmondsworth: Penguin, 1951).

Rubin, Gayle, 'The Traffic in Women: notes on the "political economy" of sex', in Rayna R. Reiter (ed.), *Towards an Anthropology of Women* (New York and London: Monthly Review Press, 1975), pp. 157–210.

Schleiner, Winfried, ' "Divina virago": Queen Elizabeth as an Amazon', *Studies in Philology*, 75 (1978), pp. 163–80.

Seneca, *Phaedra*, in *Four Tragedies and Octavia*, trans. E. F. Watling (Harmondsworth: Penguin, 1966).

Spenser, Edmund, *The Faerie Queene*, ed. A. C. Hamilton (1977; London and New York: Longman, 1980).

——*The Yale Edition of the Shorter Poems of Edmund Spenser*, eds William A. Oram *et al.* (New Haven and London: Yale University Press, 1989).

Spurgeon, Caroline F. E., *Keats's Shakespeare: a descriptive study* (1928; Oxford: Clarendon, 1966).

Strong, Sir Roy, *Gloriana: the portraits of Queen Elizabeth I* (London: Thames and Hudson, 1987).

Traub, Valerie, 'The (In)significance of "Lesbian" desire in early modern England', in Susan Zimmerman (ed.), *Erotic Politics: desire on the renaissance stage* (New York and London: Routledge, 1992), pp. 150–69.

Williams, Penry, 'Court and Polity under Elizabeth I', *Bulletin of the John Rylands Library of Manchester* 65:2 (Spring 1983), pp. 259–86.

Index